FIRST TO FIGHT

First to Fight

Henry Mihesuah

EDITED BY

Devon Abbott Mihesuah

University of Nebraska Press

Lincoln and London

Library of Congress Cataloging-in-Publication Data
Mihesuah, Henry.
First to fight / Henry Mihesuah ; edited by Devon Abbott Mihesuah.
p. cm.—(American Indian lives)
Includes bibliographical references and index.
ISBN 0-8032-3222-5 (cl : alk. paper)
1. Mihesuah, Henry.   2. Comanche Indians—Biography.   3. Comanche
Indians—History—20th century.   4. Comanche Indians—Social conditions.
5. Land tenure—Government policy—Oklahoma—Duncan.
6. Duncan (Okla.)—History—20th century.
I. Mihesuah, Devon A. (Devon Abbott), 1957–   II. Title.   III. Series.
E99.C85 M54 2002
876.6004'9745—dc21
2002022324

To all of Mihesuah's relations.

Contents

Illustrations

Introduction

Henry Mihesuah is NU MU NUU (pronounced "numina"), a Comanche of the Quahada Band. He also is my father-in-law. I do believe that writing biographies is often a nosy endeavor, and for over ten years I resisted requests by his side of the family to document his stories. Even though he is my relative who also happens to be a full-blood Comanche with a fascinating past, I thought that writing a book on him would appear opportunistic on my part. Originally, I intended to document his life for the benefit of our family, but friends have convinced me that people outside the family would also be interested in his life.

Henry (or Charlie, as his wife, Fern, and I call him—most of his friends call him "Chockie") has had a full and complex life. His myriad vignettes of growing up on his family's allotment outside of Duncan, Oklahoma, and of surviving the depression, World War II as a Marine, and relocation to California, then moving back to Oklahoma and being forced to deal with taivos (whites) who desire his land are entertaining and moving. Henry's life is also notable because of his direct link to prominent Comanches, namely his grandfather Mihesuah (pronounced "My-he-sue-ah"); his great uncle, the medicine man Eschiti (originally known as Quenatosavit, or White Eagle); and Mihesuah's frequent companion, Quanah Parker. Although Henry's stories are supplemented with discussions about Comanche history and culture, it is not the intent of this book to chronicle the Comanche past or to analyze the tribe's social, cultural, or political situations.[1]

Henry's life is also interesting to me, of course, because I'm married to his son, Joshua. But the events in Henry's life and his ancestral and immediate family also bring to light timely issues, particularly the complexity of Indian identity and the persistence of one's connection to family and tribe. Henry has various allegiances: certainly to his family, but also to the Comanche Nation, to Oklahoma, to the United States, and to the Marines. Henry's parents spoke fluent Comanche. After their experiences in boarding schools and with missionaries, however, they decided it best to limit their children's education in Comanche culture and language in hopes that Henry and his brothers and sisters could survive in the white world. Now, at age seventy-nine, Henry is attempting to learn more of his language and fill in gaps in his Comanche cultural knowledge by attending language classes and participating in tribally sponsored trips such as the 1998 visit to Palo Duro Canyon in the Texas Panhandle (the site of the 1874 Battle of Adobe Walls) and to Idaho, where Henry and other Comanches met their distant relatives—members of the Shoshone tribe.

Henry's appearance is distinctly Comanche; there is no mistaking him for anything other than a Native. He is a large man, around six-foot-three with a fifty-inch chest and a prominent profile. He prefers to wear his hair short, like he did in the Marines, and he typically dresses in a work shirt, jeans, and running shoes. He has a heavy leg brace supporting his knee, which was critically injured in car accident thirty years ago. His gimmy hats and jackets sport the logos of the Comanche Nation and the Marines.

Henry's role as a modern-day warrior, that is, as a Marine and a champion of education and self-sufficiency, continues his family tradition. And so does the newer generation. His son, Joshua, has served as president of the board of the Flagstaff United School District and president of the board of Native Americans for Community Action, in Flagstaff; he is currently director of Northern Arizona University's Native American Student Services. Henry's daughter, Adele, is a supervisory personnel specialist at the Lawton Indian Hospital, in Oklahoma, and has held the same position at the Claremore Indian Hospital and the Carl Albert Indian Hospital, both in Oklahoma, and the Cherokee Indian Hospital in North Carolina. The birth present to my son, Tanner Toshaway, from his Aunt Adele is a painting of the Eschiti war shield, and my husband Josh's present to all of us was to enlist the talents of his cousin Leonard "Black Moon" Riddles to paint his interpretation of a photograph of Mihesuah and Quanah Parker together on horseback dressed in full warfare regalia.[2] Henry's ancestors do indeed have a rich history of defending their lands, families, and name.

Crow Creek Sioux writer Elizabeth Cook-Lynn expresses her concerns about this "American Indian Lives" series in her essay "American Indian Intellectualism and the New Indian Story."[3] She claims that most subjects are "quite unremarkable." Henry is not, probably to Cook-Lynn's relief, a redeemed drunk, a grandfather as legendary figure (presented on a pedestal), a victim of racist America, or a mixed-blood outcast. As the writer of this introduction and editor of his stories, I do not consider him my fantasy of an "Indian non-conformist to American cultural restrictions." I have no illusions about Henry, and neither he nor I claim that this book is anything but a series of interesting reminisces of the life of an elder Native possessing a tremendous amount of inner strength. This book might be of use to readers wanting to understand what it is to be Indian in modern America. Henry might disappoint people Cook-Lynn refers to as "voyeurs," those who want to know intimate details of tribal life. Henry reveals no tribal secrets, gives no Comanche medicinal recipes, and describes no ceremonies except a peyote ceremony he witnessed as a child. And even then, he does not reveal anything that outsiders have no business knowing. Henry would never offer any apologies for not being more culturally Comanche, nor does he offer regret for not living in a "tribal" setting. In fact, the majority of Indians do not. Just as tribes differ from each other in history and cultural adherence, individual tribespeople vary within the same tribe. Henry's life stories are only some of the many Comanche stories waiting to be chronicled.

In 1990, anthropologist James Clifton published the anthology *The Invented Indian: Cultural Fictions and Government Policies*, in which he and his contributors express undisguised disappointment over the reality that modern Indians do not live and look like their ancestors. Standing Rock Sioux scholar Vince Deloria Jr. describes the attitude of the non-Indian contributors to the anthology: "The authors, for the most part, seem to be very disappointed that modern Indians do not act like the Indians of their undergraduate textbooks or the movies they enjoyed as children, and they seem determined to attack contemporary expressions of Indian-ness as fraudulent and invalid because modern Indians fall short of their expectations. Part of the authors' goal is to excoriate Indians for not being their own ancestors and behaving as such."[4]

It is not unusual for non-Indians to be disappointed in modern-day Comanches. After all, the image most people have of Plains tribes are of lean, scantily clad men on horseback, adorned with feathers and war paint and armed with rifles, bows, arrows, and a bad attitude. Because modern Comanches no longer hunt buffalo (at least not for survival; many Comanches, Henry included, do hunt game), or dress in feathers and buckskin (except for parades or powwows), or stay physically active (many Comanches are obese), many non-Indians believe that these people cannot be Indians. Scholars pessimistically title their books *The Comanches: The Destruction of a People* (Fehrenbach 1974) and *The Last Comanche Chief: The Life and Times of Quanah*

Parker (Neeley 1995). Or, they take another approach and glorify Comanches of the past, not of the present: *Los Comanches: The Horse People 1751–1845* (Noyes 1993); *The Comanches: Lords of the South Plains* (Wallace and Hoebel 1952).

Other more insensitive authors put forth their personal prejudices by referring to Comanches only as part of the violent past of Indian—white relations: Brown and Schmitt's *Fighting Indians of the West* (1978); Charlton's *The Old Sergeant's Story: Winning the West from the Indians and Bad Men in 1870 to 1876, by Captain Robert G. Carter* (1926); Humfreville's *Twenty Years Among Our Hostile Indians* (1903); and more recently, Hamilton's *Sentinel of the Southern Plains: Fort Richardson and the Northwest Texas Frontier, 1866–1878* in which the author describes the "lurking" Comanches as living in "lairs," refers to Indian females as "squaws," and takes delight in describing Comanche atrocities without mentioning those committed by whites.[5] I distinctly remember a class I took in graduate school, "History of the American West," in which the professor informed us that "Comanches tortured their captives by burying them to their necks in dirt, then smearing their face with honey and allowing ants to eat away the skin and eyes." When I asked where he got that tidbit, he looked at me over his glasses and said, "We'll discuss this later, young lady." He never did get me that source.

The Comanches' fighting abilities and determination to survive are simultaneously admired and despised, and nowhere are these stereotypes better reflected than in the movies. *Comanche Territory* (1950), *Comanche* (1956), *Comanche Station* (1960), *The Comancheros* (1961), and *White Comanche* (1968) all deal with hostile Indians and stereotypes, but no movie rivals John Ford's *The Searchers* (1956) for shear racism and insensitivity toward Indians. Stereotypes persist about historic and modern-day Indians, Comanches included.[6] George Catlin (1796–1872), an artist who chronicled his observations of Comanches and other tribes, offers his opinion about the connection between Comanches and their horses that reflects the lengths some go to justify the stereotypes about Indians:

> The Comanchees [sic] are in stature rather low, and in person often approaching to corpulency. In their movements they are heavy and ungraceful; and on their feet, one of the most unattractive and slovenly-looking races of Indians that I have ever seen; but the moment they mount their horses, they seem at once metamorphosed, and surprise the spectator with the ease and elegance of their movements. A Comanchee [sic] on his feet is out of his element, and comparatively almost as awkward as a monkey on the

ground, without a limb or a branch to cling to; but the moment he lays his hand upon his horse, his face even becomes handsome, and he gracefully flies away like a different being.[7]

With few exceptions, scholars who write about Comanches mainly cite each other. Drawing on Catlin's commentary, historian Walter Prescott Webb, for example, asks an equally inane question about Comanches in his *The Great Plains*: "Is it not reasonable to assume that the Comanches found it necessary to become horsemen to compensate for their short legs?"[8] Considering the length of Comanche legs today, most members of the tribe reading that statement, and indeed, Catlin's comment about them resembling monkeys, would be insulted.

A prominent example of this desire to keep Indians savage and illiterate is an article on Joshua Mihesuah, Henry's father, published in 1935 in the *Duncan Weekly Eagle* newspaper. Although Joshua and his wife, Carrie, had been educated in white schools and could speak and write in English, the unknown writer preferred to replace Joshua's speaking voice with stereotypical ungrammatical and incomplete sentences. In response to the reporter's questions about Joshua being a farmer, the writer has Joshua replying: "Me walk and push plow and cultivator. Learn how to raise corn. Am farmer now—raise crops and live good. Me farmer, you printer. . . . White men try to buy farm. No sell. All mine. Raise crops, live good. No can do anything else. Just farm." When asked about his two girls receiving an education at the Arlington School in Riverside, California, Joshua supposedly said, "Me, now, I went to school two years." (The reporter embellishes the point by adding that Joshua stuck up two fingers of his "brawny fists.") "I educated in the hand; my girls they be educated in the head. Much better. Very good." The reporter then turns his attention to Joshua's wife, Carrie, who passed away several years before. In response to a question posed to her about Comanche polygamy, Carrie is supposed to have told a friend who in turn told the reporter, "Some time buck have four, five wives, all true to him—more true than one wife now."[9] The problem with these bits of dialogue is that not only did Joshua and Carrie speak fluent, grammatical English, they both were Christians, and Carrie would never have said "buck," much less supported the idea of polygamy.

Numerous people, scholars included, expect Indians to be fully aware of their cultures and speak their languages fluently. Despite his race, appearance, and connection to his tribe, a reviewer of this manuscript asserted that Henry is "an American man who happens to be a Comanche, not a Comanche man who happens to be an American." Contrary to the expectations most American have, Indians are not static; they adapt to the changing world around them, and that means they often adopt the ways of white society and leave tribal traditions behind.[10]

Henry might be considered "marginal" because of his lack of fluent cultural knowledge of his tribe. One can also say the same of most Comanches, tribal leaders, and other full-bloods. But unlike Everett Stonequists's model of a "marginal" person—one who lives a life of frustration, unable to fit comfortably into any group, Henry never feels like an outcast.[11] He is more similar to Malcolm McFee's proposed "150% Man," an individual who has comfortably absorbed cultural traits of all his heritages and can use social skills in more than one culture, thereby making him at ease and secure in his ethnic identity.[12] In the amount of time that I have spent with Henry in the past eleven years, it is clear to me that he could not care less what scholars or anyone else thinks about the amount of his cultural knowledge. Because of his blood quantum (full-blood), appearance (distinctly Comanche), and family (which possesses a strong link to the Comanche past), he sees himself as an Indian and that's that. Neither Henry nor his children tolerate stereotypes and will challenge any insulting remark about Indians.

Many readers dislike biographies that expose "dirty laundry." Henry demonstrates an eagerness to recount his life, a joy in telling his family his memories. As a family we spent hours reminiscing, crying, and laughing over past events. Henry, Fern, and Josh aired plenty of dirty linen—most that won't see print. But a concerted effort to recall one's life often does bring back unpleasantries. Guilt sometimes resurfaces, unresolved discrepancies rush forward and need to be resolved. Ultimately, Henry expressed his happiness at the opportunity to have his stories textualized for his grandchildren and other tribal members. It has been enjoyable listening to his stories and watching his son and grandchildren absorb what he has to say. Our only disappointment in producing this book was that a close relative demanded money in exchange for clarifying stories that Henry told, but after her pronouncement, we did not ask her for any information.

Harold R. Isaacs notes in his book *Idols of the Tribe* that "all such proper names, the names that people call themselves or are called, also carry with them their own heavy store of affect and usage, of past and present history; and all of it comes to bear now, as changes come, on how people see themselves or are seen."[13]

"Mihesuah" means "first to fight" in Comanche, and Josh and our son Tanner Toshaway (as will his younger sister, Ariana, whom Henry calls *avahootsu*, or bluebird) are proud to tell their friends that. Although I, too, am proud of their name, it is not mine. I preferred to keep my maiden name, Abbott, but I succumbed to my husband's wishes and added his because I know of the pride he has in the name Mihesuah. I see myself as an addition to the Mihesuah family, but certainly not a "blood member," and I make no pretense of being a "real Mihesuah." I am an enrolled member of the Choctaw Nation of Oklahoma, and there lies my identity. I have pride in my maiden name, Abbott, a family full of complex and often quirky people that my father, mother, and I have studied and documented. My children do indeed have a legacy to be proud of.

I have listened to Henry's stories for over a decade, but it was not until early 1999 that I decided to pursue his biography. I borrowed a portable recorder and carried it with me whenever we were together. We had conversations in a variety of places: at his home in Duncan, Oklahoma, at my home in Flagstaff, at cemeteries, on park benches as we watched my children play, at my picnic table when he was adjusting his bow during hunting season, and in vehicles as we drove from place to place. After he answered a question, he often would recall another event in his life that may have only been distantly pertinent, resulting in disjointed narratives. In organizing the manuscript, I put the topics together in a logical fashion. While recording Henry's stories, I did not interact with him until his memories waned, then I prompted with questions.

Like most Oklahoma Indians, Henry usually says "Indian" when speaking of Natives, even Comanches, but he will say "Comanche" if asked a pointed question about his tribe. Although debates abound among American Indians over labels, if a person addressed him as a "First Nations," "indigenous," or even "Native," he would not know to what or to whom they referred.[14] Henry also has a very thick Oklahoma accent. He also possesses a vocabulary replete with "uhs" and strings of ungrammatical phrases. I only trimmed them in a few places where the numbers of grammatical errors made reading difficult. He did not speak in any sort of undecipherable Comanche cultural context, so unlike ethnographers who must wrestle with translations I had no fear of misunderstanding him.

After I completed the arduous task of transcribing the tapes, I organized his stories and gave the manuscript to Henry and Fern to edit. Then I sent the manuscript to Gary Dunham at the University of Nebraska Press to see if I was on the right track. After receiving his suggestions, Henry and Fern filled in gaps and clarified some statements. After revising, Fern and Henry were pleased and it was up to Nebraska's readers to make their comments.

I was not bored during the formal interviews between Henry and me, and I have never been bored listening to him, looking through scrapbooks, and driving to his allotment, which he calls the "home place." I have been especially moved by the number of graves of small children and babies in his family cemetery. As a mother, it is hard to imagine losing a child, but it was common during the first part of the twentieth century for youngsters to die from diseases and small ills that can easily be cured today. Henry is very sentimental, and it is difficult for him every time he sees his first child's grave. Some high-school students once ruined many of the headstones, just like they did at the Deyo Mission cemetery, but Henry and his relatives have restored the cemetery and maintain it.

Henry does not recall many events of his toddler days. Fortunately for us, a white girl, Lorine Gibson, lived on his Aunt Peahbo's allotment when Henry was an infant and young boy. When Lorine grew older, she documented her life in an unpublished manuscript, *A Plains Family*, which includes several intriguing observations about the Mihesuah family. As per her wishes, after Lorine died a few years ago her ashes were scattered across the Eschiti family cemetery. I appreciate that her daughter, Judy Kohler, has allowed me to include some excerpts of her mother's remembrances in the notes.

As we grow older, many times we wish we had listened to our parents and elder relatives. After they have gone, we realize it is too late. While listening to Henry, I wish I had been more attentive to my late father and my grandparents. Family frames us. We are part of all who have preceded us, and I am happy and relieved that Henry has told his stories for his descendants.

FIRST TO FIGHT

CHAPTER ONE

Family

Henry Mihesuah is a proud member of the Comanche Nation, the tribe also known as NƱ MƱ NƱƱ, "The People." They also have been called "Lords of the South Plains" because of the wide expanse they once dominated and because of their prowess at raising and riding horses.

Scholars and many Comanches posit that the Comanches were at one time a part of the Eastern Shoshones, but there exist several versions of how they separated. One version states that a single group originally lived along the Gila River in Arizona. Around 500 B.C., some, known as the Sevier Complex, migrated north to Utah, where they hunted and grew corn, beans, and squash. During a drought in the thirteenth century, they moved further north to the Great Basin, north of the Great Salt Lake. Here they were called Shoshones. Some moved to the Rocky Mountain areas of Wyoming and Colorado, where they gathered berries and roots, occasionally killed small game, and acquired horses. These people eventually became known as Comanches.[1]

Another version of the separation of Comanches and Shoshones is that while living in the Great Basin, the group divided into two factions over a dispute involving the distribution of a bear they killed. The two factions separated: the one that traveled north became Shoshones, and the one that moved south became Comanches. Still another account has it that the single group was ravaged by disease, and one of the group's leaders ordered the people to separate into smaller groups and move away in hopes that the disease would not kill everyone. Those that did not travel died.[2]

The acquisition of horses in the late seventeenth century changed the Comanches' culture. They became mobile, moving south into New Mexico and toward the Arkansas River, into the territory of the plains Apaches. They hunted buffalo, raided other tribes, and became the dominant tribe from northern Kansas to central Texas.

Comanches became skilled riders and horse breeders and tended large herds. They were predominantly raiders and hunters of the bison that ran across their domain, although they also traded horses. After a smallpox epidemic killed almost half their population in the early 1780s, Comanches allied with Kiowas, who became their raiding partners.[3] Despite their population loss, Comanches became such fearsome raiders that in 1786 the Spanish negotiated a peace policy with them. This resulted in a few decades of peace with the Spanish in New Mexico, but it did not stop Comanche raids into Mexico and later into Texas, where they effectively prevented Spanish colonization. Comanches also raided Navajos, Pueblos, Apaches, Pawnees, and Osages, and they were viewed with trepidation by most tribes and certainly by non-Indians.

By 1850, Comanches appeared to have been separated into three groups: the northern group, which stayed by the Red River in winter and ranged across the plains the rest of the year; the middle group, which hunted buffalo toward the Arkansas River in summer and wintered in Texas; and the southern group, which lived between the Colorado and Red Rivers. All of these Comanches faced a variety of enemies in the middle of the nineteenth century. A cholera outbreak devastated them in 1849; throughout the 1840s and 1850s, they fought Texans who were determined to exterminate all tribes, and they also fought other tribes over contested lands. The Comanches defeated Kit Carson in 1864 and signed a treaty in 1865 that provided them with a large portion of western Indian Territory. Whites continued to encroach onto their lands, however, and Indians were determined to keep them out. In October 1867, many Comanches signed the Treaty of Medicine Lodge Creek, which presented Comanches, Kiowa Apaches, and Kiowas with a reservation located between the Red and Washita Rivers and allowed them to hunt outside the reservation boundaries.

The Treaty of Medicine Lodge Creek was supposed to bring peace between tribes of the southern plains and non-Indians. It stipulated that tribes could hunt south of the Arkansas River and that they would receive annuities for thirty years. Tribes also were supposed to put their children in school and to learn to farm, two requirements they did not particularly relish. But because they could hunt buffalo, tribes signed. Two years later most had settled on the reserve.

Life on the reservation was depressing for Comanches; poor medical services and substandard rations caused many to become poverty-stricken and depressed. Because of their dire situation, many reservation Indians, along with Indians who refused to sign the treaty, raided Texas ranchers. Two of the men who refused to adhere to the treaty were Henry's grandfather Mihesuah (c. 1845–1912) and his friend Quanah Parker (1845–1911, the son of Cynthia

Ann Parker, a white woman captured by Comanches in 1836, and Peta Nocona, a Comanche).[4] Both men were members of the Quahada band, which means "antelope eaters."

The tide of white expansion and racism continued to batter tribes. By the 1860s, the Comanches, as well as other Indians on the plains, were aware that their major food source—bison—were being slaughtered by the thousands by white hunters, who usually took only the hides and tongues and left the carcasses to rot. After the massacre at Sand Creek in 1868, when the Methodist minister Chivington and his troops destroyed Black Kettle's Cheyennes, some twenty-five hundred Comanches surrendered and were eventually placed at Fort Sill. Other Comanches remained on the plains in a vain attempt to live traditionally. However, with the buffalo almost gone and whites swarming throughout the area, Comanches became determined to drive the intruders from their lands.

On the Staked Plains of the Texas Panhandle (on the Canadian River), white hunters established a base camp alongside the buffalo skinners at the abandoned trading post called Adobe Walls.[5] On June 26, 1874, seven hundred Indians, including Comanches and allied Arapahoes, Kiowas, Kiowa Apaches, and Southern Cheyennes, attempted to overtake the hunters at Adobe Walls. Despite their overwhelming numbers, the Indian force could not defeat the hunters. Among the warriors wounded in the battle was Mihesuah, shot through the waist. According to the Mihesuah family, Mihesuah's friend Quanah Parker helped to save him.[6]

Also present at the Battle of Adobe Walls was the Comanche medicine man and Henry's great uncle, White Eagle, a man whom many Comanches believed held magical powers. According to various sources, White Eagle asserted to that God had spoken to him, telling him that in order for Comanches to retain their land and culture they must fight and kill whites. In addition, White Eagle asserted that the tribe must perform the Sun Dance (a northern plains ritual) and that the Comanches would be unharmed if they painted themselves with White Eagle's bullet-proof paint. The belief that supernatural powers would assist them was not uncommon among tribes. Because of population loss from disease and warfare, cultural confusion, the loss of land and animals upon which they depended for survival, and subsequent depression and frustration, many tribes turned to prophets who promised better times.[7]

Because of their loss at Adobe Walls, angry Comanches renamed the disgraced White Eagle "Eschiti," meaning "coyote rectum." (Eschiti's excuse was that his medicine failed him because he encountered a skunk prior to the battle.) Every book that discusses Comanches at Adobe Walls, however, incorrectly refers to White Eagle as "Isa-tai," "Eeshatai," or "Ishatai" prior to the battle and prior to his re-christening.[8]

After the Comanches' defeat (and the demise of the bison), the noted "Indian fighter" Colonel Ronald Slidell Mackenzie (known to the tribes as Mangomhente, or "bad hand," because he lost two fingers during the Civil War) of the Fourth Cavalry attacked the Comanches' stronghold in Palo Duro Canyon.[9] Led by Tonkawa trackers, Mackenzie and his men descended into the canyon. After the Comanches escaped on foot, Mackenzie slaughtered at least fifteen hundred of the tribe's horses, burned their tipis, and confiscated their supplies. Demoralized and facing a lack of food (not because they were defeated in combat, however), the tribe surrendered at Fort Sill. They were disallowed from continuing their nomadic lifestyle, and whites settled the region at a greater rate than ever. Quanah Parker held out the longest, refusing to surrender until June 1875.

Parker eventually became a successful cattle rancher. Because Parker traveled to Washington, DC, in 1884 with Texas ranchers including Charles Goodnight and Burk Burnett in an effort to arrange a legal leasing system, Burnett built a large two-story home for Parker and his wives. White housekeepers maintained the property. Until his death in 1911, Parker hosted numerous notable guests such as President Theodore Roosevelt, Texas cattle barons, Geronimo, tribal chiefs Lone Wolf and Big Tree, and U.S. Army generals such as Hugh Scott and Nelson Miles. Quanah is also known for the role he supposedly played in bringing news of the peyote religion (the Native American Church) to the Southwest.[10]

Mihesuah had two sons. One, Henry's father, chose the name Mihesuah after his father, and his other brother chose the name Topetchy, their mother's name. Henry is not sure how many sisters Mihesuah had, but one thing is certain: the families that have emerged from these men and women have remained complicated.

HENRY

Mihesuah and Quanah were always together and going on war parties. Dad told me that whenever they'd go on parties they'd be gone two or three weeks, maybe longer. Then they'd come back and maybe they'd bring a couple of kids back from raiding ranches or someplace else. White kids and Mexicans. We have some Kiowa relatives because once, two Mexican girls got kidnapped, and the Comanches took one and the Kiowas took one. So those captives were sisters and somehow we're related through them. Anyway, the Comanches would go south, back toward Mexico and Texas and then along the Mexico line, and they'd swing further south and be gone maybe a month—the whole war party.

Mihesuah was probably like a corporal in the tribe. Dad said that Mihesuah and Quanah always watched each other in battle, that they fought together and watched each other's backs. The Comanches fought a lot, but they were smart; they didn't fight big groups. They were out there raiding, but they were also protecting what few buffalo were left. Mihesuah means "first to fight," and I think that says it all. My grandpa protected the tribe no matter what. I don't like people calling my grandpa or Quanah savages.

I saw Quanah when I was growing up but didn't think much about it. I saw his family, too. My dad saw Quanah a lot but rarely talked about him. He wasn't as much of a big deal then as he is now—everyone thinks he was a big chief.[11] We considered him a member of the family. Dad told me that once when he was little, he and his family crossed the Red River in a wagon, and it was hard because the water ran real fast. Dad had a bow and arrows with him. Quanah was in the wagon and Dad asked if he could drive the wagon across the river and he said, no, he was too little. Then Dad got mad and took out his bow and an arrow and threatened to shoot him if he didn't let him drive. Everybody thought that was pretty funny so they let Dad sit in Quanah's lap and he got to drive.

People never talked about Quanah much, even if they knew him. Indians always came to our house to visit, but his name didn't come up too many times. Nowadays it seems that everyone tries to claim they're related to him.

Mihesuah got shot at Adobe Walls. That was where Comanches and Cheyennes fought buffalo hunters who killed their food. They had signed that Medicine Lodge Treaty, and according to the agreement, whites weren't supposed to build on Comanche land that was between the Arkansas and Canadian Rivers, but they did. So the tribes decided to do something about it. The Cheyennes didn't hold their fire like they were supposed to and they went in there and started shooting. The buffalo hunters didn't know they were coming in. I went to see Adobe Walls last summer [June 1999] to tour with the Panhandle Plains Historical Museum. I walked around and stood there looking toward the Canadian River and imagined what it was like. It was mainly flat land and a few high hills. The buffalo hunters seen them Indians coming in there, and if it wasn't for that, then the Indians would have gotten all them buffalo hunters.

During the fight there was a covered wagon standing out there by itself. My grandpa Mihesuah took his bow and lifted up the flap to look in. He didn't know that there was some youngsters hiding in there, and when he lifted the side flap they shot him and knocked him off his horse. That musket ball went through his body without hitting anything vital on the inside.

Quanah Parker and some Cheyennes came by on their horses and reached down and grabbed him and drug him between them until they got away from there. Them three young fellows in the covered wagon got killed by some other Comanches. Quanah took Mihesuah to a Cheyenne camp or somewhere and they put a knife in the fire, got it red hot, and singed his wound. And then they took a horse hair and sewed it up. My dad said that his dad had knots on each side of his rib cage where the bullet came in and out.

The Indians fought all day and part of another. We lost and before long the Comanches had to live like white people for good. The buffalo were gone, the land was almost gone, and lots of Comanches were dead.

White Eagle was supposed to have been a Comanche medicine man. My grandfather Mihesuah said that White Eagle had medicine when they went into battle at Adobe Walls, and he made medicine with bullet-proof paint so that the bullets would fall off the warriors. And then quite a few Indians got killed, and them Comanches were so mad they wanted to kill White Eagle. And then White Eagle said, "I lost my medicine when a skunk crossed my path." After the Battle of Adobe Walls, White Eagle was renamed Eschiti because the Comanches were disappointed and mad at him for making bad medicine. On his tombstone it says White Eagle. That's what most people think Eschiti means—White Eagle—but it doesn't. It means "coyote rectum." Books on Comanches say he was always called Eschiti before the battle. That's not right. Why would he have a name like that without a reason?

Eschiti was real touchy about being known as a medicine man. For example, I remember that you couldn't get around him if your hands were greasy from eating. And if he was eating, you couldn't stand or walk behind him. If you did, he'd just throw a fit and act like he was going to puke. So I never walked behind him. I was afraid to. His son Jimmy tried to be a medicine man, but there wasn't nothing to it.

There was one room at Eschiti's that we couldn't go into because he had his medicine things hanging up on the walls. I went in there once and looked around but didn't know what it all was. Jimmy Eschiti's mother was my mother's sister, Tuvette. Tuvette was married to Eschiti, and when he died, she married Mumsuki. Lots of books say Mumsuki was a medicine man, but personally I don't think he was.[12] Anyway, all the headdresses, scalps, shields, and outfits belonged to Eschiti and Mumsuki. Tuvette kept all those things in a room. You couldn't go in that room unless you washed your hands and were clean. And, you couldn't say bad words. They had a staff with scalps hanging on it and there was a war bonnet and bow. I was over there one day and Jimmie Eschiti's wife, Lena, said "put all that stuff on and I'll take your picture." And I did.

When I was in California, I told the family I wanted to buy all that and they told me, "We loaned it out to a museum in Texas." I asked where in Texas and they wouldn't tell me. I know they sold it. The shield and war bonnet are gone now. I'd like to have had them. And I would have bought them.

Eschiti's buried in the family cemetery, and he's almost been dug up twice by grave robbers thinking he was buried with all his medicine and stuff like his shield and lance. So we had to cement over his grave.

The Eschitis used to live across the creek, right across from the home place where they built a big two-story house there. Fern didn't ever know about that the house, but she dreamed about it one time. She dreamed it was a two-story house with stairways that went up around the north, and on the east side it had like a porch all the way around it. She described it to me perfectly without seeing it. I never figured out how she knew what she did. Anyway, Dad wouldn't let us kids go over there. He thought we'd get hurt or something. After the Eschitis got all this money from oil, they built another big red brick home. My grandmother wouldn't lease her land out to those oil people because she was afraid her horses would break their legs steeping into all those holes they drilled. And then the Eschitis tore this other big old house down. I don't know why they tore it down and that good-sized barn on the west side of it. They got forty-eight thousand dollars during the Depression. And that's a lot of money. And all the Indians would just go over there and loaf around because they knew they'd get to go over and eat. They knew the Eschitis wouldn't tell them to leave.

And they always gambled. Cards, like poker. And hand games. They'd put in about ten cents to play—today it's more like twenty-five dollars. They'd have sticks sometimes. It'd begin with a Comanche song, then they'd close their hands and you had to guess which hand the stick was in.

When I was growing up, I never questioned any of that like I do now. I'd love to have asked Dad and Quanah questions. But now I do question them books I read, about how they fought and how the Indians were savages and tried to kill all the buffalo hunters off, who they were trying to kill, but the Comanches were trying to preserve their own land and what they used for food. That's the reason they was fighting them people, and those hunters and white people kept a-coming, more and more.

Just sitting back thinking bout it, I wish at times that I was living back then in the old times. I believe I'd have made a good warrior. I've thought about the tall grass, riding on a horse with the grass up to your back. Now, people always have something wrong with them. Even though they live long lives, they aren't very healthy. Back then people were healthier in their minds and bodies. Some of the Comanches were short but slim. Nowadays Comanches are real fat and don't get much exercise. Probably they were slimmer then because they had to work all the time on their farms like we did. People were thin 'cause they worked and we ate fruits and vegetables and meat, and we didn't have chips and pies and junk from the grocery store like today.

Henry has fond memories of his mother, Carrie Peahbo (c. 1882–1932), who died from pneumonia when he was ten. From all reports she was a loving and deeply religious mother and friend whose home was open to less-fortunate Indians and non-Indians alike. Henry and his siblings were raised by their father, who was known simply as Mihesuah (1874–1962) until he was given the name Joshua (people pronounced it "Joshaway") by missionaries when forcibly taken to Fort Sill Indian School as a child.[13] Joshua spoke Comanche exclusively during his childhood, as did Carrie; but after arriving at school, his long braids were cut off and he was forbidden to speak Comanche. Because of the strong influence of the boarding school, Joshua did not speak much Comanche the rest of his life. And the influence of missionaries at the nearby Deyo Mission he joined caused Joshua not to encourage his children to learn Comanche customs.[14]

As discussed in numerous books on the federal boarding schools, the imposition of white culture and the severe punishment of children who attempted to speak their tribal languages made such an impression on the children that many left their traditions behind.[15] Quite often, one family member educated at a boarding school would influence the rest of his or her family to lose interest in their traditional culture or at least to investigate "white ways."

It appears that Joshua and Carrie were responsible for changing their family's cultural allegiances. The Mihesuahs were not the only Comanches to alter their worldviews. With their lands allotted by and surrounded by whites and with their traditional lifestyle of hunting gone forever, numerous Comanches converted to Christianity in the early part of the twentieth century.[16] Morris Foster notes that during this time a division developed between the "church people" and "peyote people," but he asserts that this division did not affect personal and familial associations.[17] Henry, however, believes that because his uncle Topetchy used peyote and his father was Christian, the two brothers became estranged. The Comanche community became fragmented as more became Christians, moved away to find what few jobs were available, and intermarried with non-Comanches.

Joshua realized that the only way to survive and succeed in the white man's world was to become educated—even at the expense of remaining culturally Comanche. He also knew that one of the few professions open to him was farming, a skill he learned at Fort Sill Boarding School. In 1910, Joshua was among the fifteen percent of Comanches who farmed.[18] Many Comanches could not compete financially with white farmers after 1920, but Joshua is noted for being one of the few Comanches who successfully made a living at farming until around 1938, when he became ill.

HENRY

Mihesuah died when he was sixty-eight, and my Dad was alive. When we went to visit Mihesuah we also went to see his brother, Topetchy. They came over to our place, but not a lot. Maybe we didn't see each other much because my Dad was a Christian and Mihesuah used peyote. Dad and my mother thought we'd be better off as Christians, and that's how they lived their lives. They never said anything bad about people who weren't Christians; they just pushed Christianity. They're the ones who took a big step away from Comanche traditions, and it's been hard to get back into step.[19]

Dad always told me it was sad when the Indian kids got taken away from their parents and were put in school. When he was a little kid they took him away from his folks and took him to Fort Sill Indian School. He cried and him and his brother ran off, but those army men would get them back. His parents tried to get him back. Even if Comanches thought of sneaking to the school in the middle of the night and taking their kids home, they couldn't. Back then, they took all the Indian kids from their parents, put them in school, and if you did take them, then the army would just come get them again. I imagine all the kids and their parents threw a fit but they took them anyway. The parents could even get thrown in jail. Sometimes Dad would hide, and they always found him.

After he knew he couldn't get away and finally settled in, he learned to read and write. Before he went to school he only spoke Comanche. He couldn't talk Comanche at Fort Sill 'cause they'd whup him if he did.[20] My dad had an Indian name: Automo. But they wouldn't let him use it. They cut off Dad's braids and gave him his first name from out of the bible, Joshua. Up until then, he was just Mihesuah. Everyone pronounced it "Joshaway." I named my son Joshua after him.

They made him talk English at the school. If teachers did that now, they'd probably get locked up. Dad told us that those teachers didn't care. They just picked up all the little kids and took them off to school.

School really affected him. I don't know how many years he stayed, but it was quite a while. He never talked about the importance of keeping traditions. All Dad ever talked about was how they taught him to farm and he turned out to be a good farmer. When they allotted the land out, he farmed and kept up with the white people and did better than most. Everybody back then said, "Mihesuah makes good crops." I guess that once Dad was at school a while he liked it since he wanted to learn to farm. Still, that's not right to take a child away from their parents. It's hard on a little kid.

After school, Dad raised cotton, corn, and maize on the home place. And he had a big garden, and out in front of the house they had peach and plum trees growing all over. We'd gather them plums and peaches and corn and we'd have a big fire and cook that corn with the shucks on it.

I can barely remember my mother, Carrie Peahbo. She was heavy-set, and to me she was a pretty lady. She spent all her time with us. She cooked for visitors and talked Comanche to whoever came over.[21] Mama knew how to read pretty well, and she read whatever we had in the house, but Dad never did read much. We got letters from family, but we didn't write any. I only have one picture of her. There was some guy who came around to get pictures from Indian people. He'd tell them that he'd find their families and give it to them and make duplicates. Well, he sold those pictures to magazines and museums and the people never got their pictures back. Most Indians are too trusting. He came around me once and wanted that picture of my mother, the only one I had. I told him no. I'm not sure which brother or sister that is in the cradleboard.[22]

My mother died somewheres around me being ten. Dad never remarried. I can remember when she passed away. They said she had pneumonia. A whole bunch of Indian friends came to the house 'cause we had the body there. I was ten when I went to the funeral. I walked up to the graveyard with one of my brothers. Most had old cars, and we usually rode on a wagon—a buggy. They buried her in the family cemetery, the Eschiti cemetery, that's north of the home place. I didn't go into the cemetery to the grave. I just stood on the other side of the fence. When I go out there now, I think of her. Me and Fern have a baby girl buried there—Cynthia Lee Mihesuah—she was born February 17, 1948, and died about a month later.

Dad never did marry again. There was this lady from Walters who always tried to talk to Dad—she was a pretty lady, too—but Dad didn't seem to care much about her. Maybe he missed Mom too much to marry again, or maybe he just wanted to concentrate on farming and keep food on the table, which was hard to do out there. My sisters didn't really have any women to talk to, and I wonder how that affected them growing up.

When my sister May died, her daughter Eva and my sister Hilda got the pictures. Hilda lost her pictures in a flood. Eva had said, "Uncle Chockie, you to come down here and take some of these pictures," but I never did get any. I even sent my sword back here from the war. I had Dad's bow he made me, and I also had a pistol that I used in the service. I told May, "I want you to keep these things for me." When I got back, the bow was gone and the pistol was gone. May said someone stole it, but I don't believe it. I thought I could trust them. Eva has all those pictures now and I asked her once to see them, and she had some excuse as to why I couldn't see them. So the only picture I got of my mother is from one of my cousins, Matilda Topetchy.

My parents were very religious.[23] I never heard Dad say a cuss word. He was Baptist, and we went to Deyo Indian Mission. We'd leave on a Saturday in a wagon and go to Faxon, where Dad's brother, Topetchy, lived.[24] Then Sunday morning they'd all get their horse teams and go to Deyo Mission, and they'd go to the services. And then they'd go back to Faxon and then Monday morning they'd go home. I remember about halfway from Faxon, we'd feed the horses then stop where this guy had a watering trough, and that's where we'd eat sandwiches and rest the horses and then go on home.

Indians from all tribes went to Deyo Mission. It was all Indian land. I think the missionaries were named Gilbert from New York or someplace east, and they picked that area out for a church. It was built by Rev. Deyo. Dad said that Quanah gave them permission to build there.

I got to meet kids from other tribes out there during the camp meetings. They'd come out in covered wagons. Mostly there were Comanches, but some Apaches and Kiowas. I never did pay much attention to what tribe people were from. We were all just kids. Back then, them men wore suits with long braided hair and hats and the ladies wore a shawl, but I call it a skirt, around their shoulders. I remember, if they needed to go to the restroom, the squatted down and you couldn't tell what they were doing. Mama used to do that. You could tell what the men were doing, though.[25]

The way my parents figured it, there's wasn't but only one God. They didn't look down on people who practiced the Comanche religion. They just didn't believe in it. Now, at one time they were pro–Comanche religion, but they changed on account of that Deyo Mission.[26]

When I was older the preacher at Deyo Mission asked for volunteers to be a wise man in one of them sunrise Easter pageants in the Wichita Mountains.[27]

When I was practicing being a wise man I had some hand-me-down cowboy boots, and the heels were all worn down. I had to walk and carry one of those staffs that looked like it had a bird nest on top. Anyway, they had goats that took off running and we had to round them up at night. We didn't have flashlights. We finally caught them when I used the staff with a crook to catch them. I enjoyed being a wise man.

★   ★   ★

Dad was a cowboy before he farmed. He worked on the Burkburnett ranch in Texas, west of Wichita Falls across the Red River. I don't know how many thousands of acres they had. Dad said him and a dozen other Indian cowboys ran cows and broke broncs, and for fun they'd go chase antelope and rope them from the horses. They'd follow them in relays, one horse then another horse, to wear them down. Then they'd rope them and let them go. Dad also said they'd even chase coyotes and rope 'em. But he said that was just like a sport. I imagine they had fast horses to do that. I don't know if they were Injun ponies or not. They'd run down the coyotes in the relays, too.

Dad was really healthy most of his life. I really don't know what he died from. He got sickly when he was old and may've had pneumonia. When he got older he didn't feel good and seemed like he didn't take care of himself. So he came and stayed with me and my wife, Fern.

★   ★   ★

I don't know for sure when I was born. My birth certificate says I was born July 17, 1922, but we've always gone by July 25, 'cause my sisters say the certificate's not right. I can't tell you for sure where I was born, either. They said I was born out there in the country, and some in my family say I was born in the Indian hospital in Lawton. That's what I go by. My sisters were for sure born in the Indian Hospital in Lawton.

There was Stella, Hilda, Martha, Johnny, Roy, and me. May, she was the oldest and kind of raised us, but she also bossed us. She married a Mexican guy and was Eva's mother. Eva's my niece. Martha passed away when she was seventeen or eighteen years old from pneumonia. Lots of people out there died from it. She also had excema real bad on her face.

Then there was the youngest, Wanda. She went to school there at the local Bread School then she went to Fort Sill Indian School. The problem with her was that she married a soldier out of Fort Sill. They started out drinking and that's what contributed to both their deaths, I think. He was a lot older than her. If she had taken care of herself she'd be alive today. She was always outside, working on her garden, or something, but she drank all the time.

They had two kids and they were mostly out on their own. She never was interested in Comanches much. Some of her friends were, though. A lot of them talked Comanche all the time. They were raised up different from the way we were. If we had been around people who talked Comanche all the time then maybe we would have, too. My older sisters Stella and Hilda knew how to speak Comanche pretty good. My brother Johnny did a little.

The one that drank all the time was my older brother Roy. He passed away about nineteen years ago. He finally had a family and he didn't take care of them, you know. He was always a good mechanic and good hand, but every time he'd get paid he'd go to town and spend his money and get drunk. He used to live on Uncle David's place on the next quarter south. I felt sorry for them little ones. You could talk to him all day long about how bad drinking was for him and he'd agree with you and next thing you know he'd be at it again. He just ran around all the time. Drinking anything that had moonshine in it. Looked like what you're drinking there [Sprite]. That stuff can take the top of your head off and he drank it all the time.

A lot of that drinking may have been because he was frustrated being Indian or maybe because he was bored. Roy smoked and drank and so did all his friends. After drinking they were more outgoing and they talked more, then got into trouble with someone. He had money from his job to drink and he had lots of friends, but as soon as the money was gone so were his friends. Maybe that's why I can't stand being around people who drink.

My brother Johnny was tall and slim and never did drink. Never smoked or anything. He kept telling that I should fight back whenever someone picked on me. One time when I was fifteen, Roy had been drinking at a bar in Duncan and me and Johnny came to get him. Johnny was driving an old Ford with a jump seat in the back. We were crossing Little Beaver on the old wooden bridge and Roy was up in the front seat with Johnny. Roy wanted Johnny to take him back to town and Johnny didn't want to. I was aggravating Roy 'cause I was in the back talking. Roy said, "Stop because I'm gonna whip Charlie."

And I said, "Roy, you can't whip me."

Well, Johnny stopped and we got out by the creek where the grass was high. I jumped out and went to the edge of the bank and Roy doubled up his fists and swung and I stepped out of the way and he fell into the ditch and all that Johnson grass, and Johnny said, "Get in, Let's go."

"You just gonna leave him here?" I asked.

"Yeah, he can walk. He'll find his way home."

And so we left him and eventually he came home.

Another time two guys jumped on Johnny at a dance in Duncan, and Johnny fought them guys. Whipped them both, but he almost got his thumb bit off. It got infected and he had to go to the Indian Hospital in Lawton.

This other guy who lived out there, Hoot Gann, was always drinking moonshine, too. I never did taste it, just smelled it. He also liked wine home-made with them 'possum grapes. His buddies, Levi and them colored guys like Sam Medlock, would get together and go down there by the creek and pick the grapes. They made it over there on Medlock's place. He was a colored guy who lived in a dugout back there on my uncle's place. Dug out a place in the creek bank and lived back in there. Sometimes them guys would have a wife with them, then the next week they'd be gone and another one'd be there. My dad didn't like that and he'd come out and tell them. Dad didn't allow them to bring that moonshine on the property, either.

Nobody I knew smoked except my brother Roy. He rolled his own smokes, Prince Albert or Bull Durham. I used to get a kick out of him when he tried to keep that Bull Durham lit and it kept going out. A colored guy who lived behind us in a long shotgun house smoked a pipe sometimes.

We all kept our hair short 'cause Dad did. Uncle Dave, down there south of us, he had short hair. Burt Treetop had long hair. He wasn't tall like his name. He was short and squatty.[28]

I got the name Charlie when I was a little boy. I rode my horse Skeeter all the time, and a neighbor named Charlie Boulware across the field graded the roads on the wagon and team. He'd go three or four miles and I'd just follow him around on my horse. And everybody started calling me Charlie. Some of my friends didn't know my real name. All they knew was my Dad's name, Joshaway. They didn't know his last name, just his first name, so everybody living around the home place knew me and my brothers Roy and Johnny by "Joshaway." They'd say, "that's Roy Joshaway," or "Johnny Joshaway" or "Charlie Joshaway."

I picked up my other name, Chockie, in Duncan. The people down there always called me Chockie. A Choctaw lived there where the vo-tech school is in Duncan now. His family had 160 acres north of it. I used to go to Duncan with Dad, and while he was grinding corn for bread I'd get off and play with them Choctaws. When Dad came back through he'd hang something like a handkerchief or a piece of paper on the gate and I'd know he'd gone by. I just watched the gate knowing it'd take him two or three hours or longer. A couple of time I forgot and he'd already started home and then I'd start running trying to catch him, and I lot of times I didn't catch him. I'd go through pastures and across a creek to get home. I used to run all the time in hand-me-down shoes.

Or barefooted. My feet were tough enough so the goathead stickers didn't bother me if I stepped on them.

Anyway, me and that Choctaw boy, Simy Charleston, played together, and Dad started calling me Chockie. To this day people in Walters call me Chockie. I called up my old buddy Clifford Barbie one day and he said "Who is this?"

And I said, "Henry." Lots of times I introduce myself and forget I have these other names. Henry, Charlie, and Chockie. I forget which is which.

So Clifford says, "Who is this again?"

And I said, "Chockie."

Then he says, "Why didn't you say so? I know who you are now."

CHAPTER TWO

Early Life

As the twentieth century began, Indians were seen as "vanishing red men," doomed to extinction because many of the tribes were confined to reservations, many tribes were extinct, and the Indian population had declined to approximately 125,000.[1] In the opinion of sympathetic whites, Indians who managed to survive would need to assimilate to the ways of white society, that is, become Christianized and be formally educated in white schools. In 1887, the federal General Allotment Act (also known as the Dawes Severalty Act, or the Dawes Act) was passed.[2] Many reservations and tribal lands were to be broken up into parcels and allotted to individuals or families. Heads of families most commonly received 180 acres, while individuals received 80 acres. In theory, these lands would be farmed by the increasingly civilized Indians.

Forcing Indians to become farmers was only one rationale for allotting tribal lands. After the lands had been distributed, the surplus was auctioned off to land-hungry whites. Tribes lost a total of ninety million acres, two of every three acres they possessed prior to allotment. Besides the enormous loss of tribal lands, other scandals were associated with allotment. For example, the Act was supposed to protect tribes from fraud, so allotments were to be held in a trust status for twenty-five years; by that time, it was hoped that the Indians would become acculturated, successful farmers. However, Indians were allowed to lease their lands to others, and as a result much land was destroyed by overgrazing and deforestation. Guardians (also known as "grafters") were appointed to assist minors and "incompetents" in understanding aspects of allotment; but guardians often wrote wills for their charges that bequeathed the land to the guardians themselves, and many Indians were found dead under questionable circumstances. Allotment is still seen by Indians and sympathetic whites as a failure and a ploy to further dispossess Indians of their dwindling lands.[3]

Henry's parents received allotments, and he was raised on his family's allotment on Little Beaver Creek between Duncan and Lawton, Oklahoma.[4]

Many Indians in need of money sold their allotments. Between 1907 and 1920, at least 350 allotments (approximately 80,000 acres) were sold to whites by Apaches, Comanches, Kiowas and Wichitas, and the fifteen hundred Comanches found that thirty thousand of their new neighbors were whites.[5] Henry's parents did not sell their land, but many of Henry's extended family did; Henry's allotment is now surrounded by land owned by non-Indians who are attempting to limit his access to his property. Numerous whites and blacks lived around Henry's allotment, and he states that he "was raised up with those little colored boys." Indeed, many of his happiest childhood memories involve escapades with his black friends.

In 1928, the *Meriam Report* was published by the Institute for Government Research. This lengthy study of conditions on Indian lands revealed serious problems, such as lack of self-determination, poverty, and poor health care, housing, and education. Indeed, many people were poor—including whites and blacks—yet Henry's father, Joshua, remained a successful farmer. In fact, Joshua hired black sharecroppers to help work his fields, and white neighbors called on him regularly for assistance in feeding their families.

Henry's education had a slow start, and he completed only the sixth grade. He states that he wishes his father had "busted my fanny" for letting him drop out. Today he is a staunch supporter of education and encouraged his children to earn college degrees.

In 1946, Henry married his sweetheart, Fern Teague, during boot camp leave. Henry is a full-blood Comanche and Fern is white. This union has been successful in part because of Fern's strong, confident personality. Despite opposition to their marriage by women on Henry's side, Fern has remained a stabilizing force for Henry and their two children. She has shown admirable patience in their "mixed-race" marriage, persevering through wartime, the death of their first child, relocation to California, and more currently, Henry's extended hunting trips.

HENRY

I farmed with my dad and my brothers, Roy and Johnny. We used to work hard on that farm. We'd go outside early every morning and shuck corn. All we had was a kerosene lantern to see. Man, it was cold some mornings shucking corn for those hogs. Mice and rats ran everyplace. Then we milked the cows. Those little calves, we had to get them away from their mothers for a few minutes so we could milk. If the calves were still in the pen when Dad went out there, we got lectured. A lot of times they'd go and start sucking their mothers and the mothers wouldn't have enough milk for us. Their udders would get dry and chapped and bleed, you know. We'd get some beef taller and put on the udders, rubbed it in good and the body heat melted it, and that'd help. We didn't have no money for anything else so we used that and it worked fine.

While one of us was milking the other might go slop the hogs, then carry water to them. That was a lot of work to do before we even left for school. Roy wasn't too much help, but Johnny was pretty handy. Then we went in the house to get something to eat. We took our lunch to school in a gallon bucket.

We had a wood-burning stove and got the wood from trees that had fallen next to the creek. Me and my brothers'd take that team of horses down there and load it up with long wood and stack it, and then in the evening after school we'd go out and cut enough to last the next day. Cottonwood and elm burns better. Cottonwood burns hot but doesn't last very long. Also mulberry. At night I'd cut wood and get it ready for the next day, and me and Wanda had an old wheelbarrow to collect it. Stella kept after us to go do it 'cause it was getting later in the evening. We had one room, like a junk room, where we kept the wood and kindling where it could dry. One night Dad was sitting in the other room and came in there when he heard me and Wanda arguing back and forth about who was supposed to stack the wood. Dad reached over there and picked up a stick of wood. He threw it and hit me in the head with that thing while I was running away from him, and from that time on, I never argued about stacking wood.

Dad was one of the main farmers out there. We rotated our crops. One year we'd grow cotton in one place and then the next year it'd be corn. We had all that stuff growing at once. About eighty acres worth. We also planted across the creek on Hilda and Stella's place that used to be our mother's allotment. There was a bridge across the Little Beaver. So we just went across there and harvested. We depended on the rain 'cause we didn't water the crops ourselves. Sometimes they burned up for lack of water. It's not like now when you can get farmer's insurance. We sold the cotton and corn, and if we had a good crop, then that would pay for the seeds and other equipment. We also had turkeys, chickens, hogs. Lots of hawks flew around. We didn't have a tractor. All we had were a team of horses and a single plow to break that land with. And we followed the plow with two handles and a strap around our neck all day long. Like pushing a wheelbarrow.

Didn't have no combines then, so we had to go down through the head-high rows with a team of horses and a wagon and cut it off by hand. Never did fertilize. The corn was almost head-high, and we got sore hands harvesting it. We just cut off the heads and threw them in the wagon. The only time Dad got on me was when we were gathering corn out there—it was a "down row"—and

I got behind and they had to help me catch up. We had a team of horses and wagon that would go over the corn and it would fall down and then we'd pick the corn. Once, Dad and Johnny took three rows at a time on each side of the wagon and I had one row and didn't keep up 'cause I was goofing around. Dad kept after me and I kept messing around, not paying attention, and Dad hit me in the head with an ear of corn. He would've made a good ballplayer. I saw him kill a quail with an ear of corn.

Usually we raised so much corn that the granary was full and so was our big barn. So we took hog wire and built a fence around it and put corn in it. Then we had to shuck all that by hand. We had this little machine set up about as big around as a small plate. We put that corn down in there and turned it to shell the corn. Worms and all got shelled, although they were mainly dried out. People'd come who didn't have the money and they'd swap hogs or something for corn. Or work. Dad always had something for them to do, like build the fence.

Dad got credit at a place called Kirby's. He'd go up there and get credit, and then whenever he got his crop he sold it and paid off his debt. I can remember one time when Ralph and I went in and that guy's son started cussing Dad for not paying his bill. Well, I never heard Dad say a cuss word back, and of course he'd already paid the bill on time. The guy just wanted to gripe.

Dad got the lumber for the house and barn from Duncan and he hauled the wood in a wagon pulled by teams. He and some of his friends built both.[6] It's not like now. Back then when someone needed help, everyone came and they built a house and barn. Today, people say, "Yeah, I'll come help if you pay me." Like if somebody got sick, then all the neighbors would come over and help pick his crops till he got well.

This one guy—he was a carpenter—helped us build the barn twice after it got blown down by tornadoes. Another white guy named Charlie Fouty came in and helped build a few things on the property, like the sitting room in the back.

Had a barn there, big enough that we had a basketball court in it. The foundation's still there. One summer a tornado hit it and then one knocked it down again; that was twice in the early forties. Didn't do anything to the house, didn't even break a window. But it blew straw into the west wall so hard that it stuck straight out. I guess that wind was so strong it just twisted that straw so it went right into the wood. Plucked the chickens clean and blew my cow across the creek. Didn't kill her or the hogs. We were inside the cellar and that door was just rattling. Then another tornado blew the top part of my sister's house away.

I went out to my old cellar the other day and it's spooky. Probably big old snakes and spiders down there. Anyway, we rebuilt the barn from the scraps and wood brought in on wagons and teams from Duncan, and it got blown down again. Charlie Fouty, he was a carpenter and helped rebuild it. The roof was really steep, and he and his helpers looked like spiders crawling around working on it.

When we all moved out a long time later all the furniture was taken by family who won't say they have it. When we lived there, there weren't many trees around the house, but now it's all grown up with mesquite and other stuff.

When I was eight I was playing in front of the house about four feet from the steps with a little train made out of metal. Stella, Martha, and all them were in the cellar 'cause of a thunderstorm. Stella tried to get me in the cellar and I didn't pay attention to them and the next thing I knew I woke up in the cellar. Lightning had struck me. When I woke up in the cellar my sisters were crying 'cause they thought it killed me. We had lightning rods around the ridges of the house about as big around as my thumb. They probably saved me 'cause most of the bolt went into the ground. Lightning hit one of the rods and burned holes through it. I don't know why they weren't set up away from the house. I told Fern the other day that that could have messed my brain up. It sure could have.

★   ★   ★

That Dust Bowl was in the twenties and thirties.[7] It didn't affect us like it did the people west of us, but man, it was dry. Didn't make any money those years. Our well never went dry though, and there's still water in it. Everyone else's well went dry and came to get water from us. We dropped a rope and pulley to get water then pulled it back up. We watered cows from it. Once we had a windmill. If it got dry out there we used water from the creek. That was a good day-long job, watering them crops, the horses, and cows. Most of the time we depended on the rain for the plants. Lots of time we lost our crops. Back there then, it wasn't like now. We could tell if it was winter, spring, summer, and fall. It just come natural. But like now, we don't know when we're gonna have a spring or a fall—it just goes right on through. All the automobiles, refineries, all over the world are changing the environment. That has a lot to do with it. Even trees are dying.

The creek dried up during that time, too. When it was running I fished it a lot. During the Depression we grew our own food and would butcher a steer, then can it. Everybody canned beef and tomatoes and other vegetables. We put the canned goods and potatoes down in the cellar and we'd eat that through the winter. We growed cotton, corn, maize, all kinds of stuff like pumpkins and tomatoes. Killed a hog, they'd salt it down and put it in the smokehouse. Everything we canned lasted a long time. Corn, tomatoes, meat, fish. We'd save the lard from the hogs and put it in the big cast-iron pots. We'd make chitlins—hog rinds, the fat from the skin—and save the grease from it. They'd also cure the hogs by putting brown sugar on their shoulders and back and hind legs, and then it'd keep in the smokehouse.

One white guy named Honey Bee Jackson kept bees. He'd come down to the home place and look for water on the ground 'cause the honeybees come to drink from it, and then he'd follow them. That's the way he found their hives. Then he'd ask Dad if he could get the honey, and Dad said okay, if we got some, too. Then Jackson'd cut down part of the tree. He wore a net over his head and shoulders and he'd light a little fire with green leaves to make smoke so the bees wouldn't sting him.

Aunt Tuvette had about forty Indian ponies. Mustangs. She said to me, "You go find you a horse," 'cause I had an old work horse I rode. "Any one you catch, you keep it," she said.

So I went out there and tried to catch one. Me and my friends would try to wear them out, but we never could catch one. So through the winter we started feeding them. When one came into the barn, we closed the gate and caught him. So then we went in and had a rodeo breaking him and after that I rode him all the time. But he wouldn't let nobody ride him but me.

★　★　★

I first hunted with a bow. Dad made me a bow and some arrows, and it took him a while to make that stuff. Made the bow out of bois d'arc wood [Osage-orange] and the string from sinew. That tree with the big, round green fruit things bigger than tennis balls. He made arrows out of dogwood and turkey feathers. I'd ride my horse and shoot rabbits off the horse with my bow and arrows. We didn't have those field thorns like they do now. The only thing they had was a point carved on the arrow. I had dogs, and me and them little colored boys would go hunting and fishing down on the creek after we finished our work.

I taught myself to hunt and taught myself how to butcher too. If I went with anyone it was one of those colored boys that lived near us. There weren't any deer out there then when I was growing up. No wild turkeys. Only thing out there were cottontails, jackrabbits, coons, possum, and maybe a bobcat, and lots of coyotes. Squirrels, quail, lots of snakes, too. Everybody called them coyotes "wolves," but they're not.

As far as butchering, when I was little like Ari and Tosh I used to go out there with Dad and after he killed a cow or steer, and then everybody from all over came out there. Nothing goes to waste, you know. That's how I learned to butcher. When I was about seven they had the entrails in a big tub and they'd turn those entrails inside out and wash all that stuff out of them then boil it and we'd eat it. We called it quetucks.

When I was small I always wanted to go fishing or hunting instead of helping around the home place. If those colored boys weren't around Dad sent somebody with me, usually Stella, 'cause I was too small to go by myself. I had five or six dogs. And I had a slingshot. We'd go down there, and the first thing I'd do is lose Stella, and she'd go back to the house, which would suit me, so then I could hunt by myself with my dogs. Neighbors'd have puppies and we'd always get one. Those dogs were regular old cur dogs.

As I got older and when I had a little money I could afford to go hunting with friends and better equipment. In the forties or fifties I went with friends like Fred Hamilton, who was a building contractor. He was out around our land a lot. I got to know him, and he'd hire me and my buddy Dee Westbrook to work for him. We'd also go hunting elk and deer.

Back then there were lots of rabbits and squirrels. There were jackrabbits everywhere. They were so thick they'd eat up the cotton everyone planted. I remember Dad had to go out and replant all that cotton.

We had lots of farm animals around the place. Those turkeys weren't too smart. The little ones would stay out in a storm and drown. Their mothers tried to round them up and couldn't. We tried to catch them too, but we'd step on some of them. We had about seventy-five head all the time. We'd herd them out in the cotton fields where there were all kinds of bugs out there, grasshoppers especially. The turkeys fed all the way to the end of one row then we'd herd them back again down the other side. Then when we got to one side by the creek, they wanted to go to water, so we had to let them go until they came back home. Then we'd do it again the next day. The turkeys didn't have many predators back then when there were people on every quarter land with five or six kids and their dogs. Not like now when you can wander for two miles and nobody's living there. There weren't many varmints, and everybody had dogs to keep them away. We sold the turkeys in the fall around Thanksgiving so we'd have money for clothes, books, and Christmas presents.

Lots of barn owls stayed in the barn and caught mice. We also had them little sqweech [screech] owls. Dad always said not to let them get around the house because they're an omen that something bad's gonna happen. Any time we heard one next to the house all us kids had to run out there and scare him off. I never saw anything bad that happened after a sqweech owl was at the house, but Dad always said it could, and he looked over his shoulder a lot when owls were around. Them big old barn owls lived around the house, too. They were about a foot high with them big old eyes and white feathers. We never bothered them. And those other owls, like those horned owls, weren't supposed to be dangerous either. When we got a bunch of pigeons, us and some colored friends living on the home place would catch them and eat 'em. That's how we kept the pigeons thinned down.

We also had lots of snakes. We never did have problems with them except down by the pond. A cow sometimes stepped on a water moccasin and would get bit, then their legs would swell up on them. So we killed the snakes with a shotgun, or most of the time a slingshot. Those big old black snakes—bull snakes—were out there in the barn. We didn't pay too much attention to them. One time when I was about fifteen I had on an old leather jacket and was gonna throw some hay out to feed the horses. I'd go out in the mornings and evenings to move it around by the light of a kerosene lantern where we could get to it in the mornings. Well, I was up on the hay trough so I could throw down the hay and there was a ledge about a foot wide all the way around it. I felt something hitting my shoulder and I swatted at whatever it was and turned and saw this big bull snake next to my head trying to bite me. I killed him because he scared me so bad.

Sometimes animals got rabies. Dogs mainly, and I can remember one cow got it. I don't know how many times they had to shoot it before they killed it. It was miserable, staggering and slobbering. Then Dad and them made a big bonfire and burned that cow. They wouldn't let us mess around near it, so I don't know if it smelled good or not.

A friend of mine, Toby Vowell, was down by the creek one day and found this little kitten. Someone had dumped him out in the creek and he found him. One day when I was out wandering around out there I came by there and him and his dog were out there working. He had a little box and I asked him if it was a trap. Toby said he was building a little cat house. He said, "Someone throwed that cat away. And I've been bringing food down here for it."

Then I said, "Something's gonna catch that cat." He was a little thing, not wild.

So the next time I come by the box was gone and I figured something killed the cat. The next time I saw Toby he was driving his old Chevy down by the creek. And I asked, "What happened to your box?"

He said, "Charlie, you said something was gonna get him so I took him home and he's in my house."

Most of us didn't like throwing animals away like that. Toby was all upset that someone threw him away and he wanted to take care of it. It's still thataway; people do that all the time to animals.

★ ★ ★

We had all kinds of friends. White, colored, everybody. I was raised up with colored boys during the Depression, when everything was bad, nobody had work, no jobs. There were three colored families, and they had a bunch of little kids that I played with. I have one picture and you can't tell the difference between me and the colored boys; I'm just as dark as they are 'cause I stayed in the sun all the time.

My dad had three houses on the home place and he'd let the colored people come out and live in the houses for free, and he'd give them a milk cow and let them have a garden, and they in turn helped Dad around the farm. They didn't have anywhere to go. Dad let them stay there because they were starving. Just like when they lived in town, they didn't have nothing. Sometimes they'd go out and find a job, and they'd move back to where they came from and more people'd come out. Nobody helped other people like my Dad did. Dad fed whoever came out there.

They were so poor they just couldn't even get a tom turkey and several females and start raising their own. They couldn't even get credit for cotton seed. A lot of times, they'd come to the house and Dad'd give them something to eat. He'd get corn and give it away. When Dad crossed other people's land, he'd give seed to the people who didn't have nothing. Sometimes, if people wanted to get seed so they could plant crops, they'd go up to granary and try to get credit. If they couldn't get credit there then they'd try the banker, and he might loan them enough money for some seed. If the crops grew, then they paid him off. We didn't have to do that; we'd shell corn and then go plant it.

Dad would let them live on our place, but there wasn't no drinking allowed, no fighting or anything like that. Then if they did, he'd tell them they were getting loud. Then, if he had to tell them again, they'd stop because they couldn't afford to move.

Most of those people around us were white people. Those whites didn't know anything about Comanches. They were on the allotted land because the Indians moved out and let them sharecrop it. The Indians wouldn't work it, so they'd go off and scrounge off of other Indians someplace else. Then if the food ran out, they'd go off to another Indian.

Like today, they use what the tribe gives them. There's some people that just live plum off the tribe. Lots are unemployed. And some live off welfare at the same time they get money from the tribe. We're paying for those people on welfare. You can't get food stamps and Comanche commodities at the same time, 'cause the government checks.

Whites scrounged off the Indians, too. I can remember one time this Anderson family came to get some corn from us. Dad always knew exactly how many turkeys we had, just like you know how many chickens you have out there in your yard. Well, one was missing after they left and Dad knew it was gone. One day Dad was waiting for them, and they had a turkey tied onto the side of the cab. So he told them, "You got my turkey, I see it. You take him, but don't you come back no more." He'd help people, but wouldn't tolerate stealing.

My parents also had other Comanches coming over all the time. They for sure came over whenever we had a crop picked or killed a beef. And sometimes they came to visit along with the white and colored people. Dad would have a big crop of corn or something, and all the Indians would come over and we'd light some big fires and cook that corn. They'd cook it and take a knife and cut the kernels off, and then they'd dry it for their soup. Some came over with wagons meaning to haul corn home, and the people who came over to visit and help Dad got to take home some.

Those Comanches who lived around us looked, you know, normal. Some were heavy-set and some were short, but most were tall and slim. Quite a few of the men had long hair they braided. Women wore their hair all different ways. Some braided it, but a few kept it short.

A lot of our Comanche neighbors never spoke English. I guess they never learned how. Like this one lady, our Aunt Tuseda, who died twelve years ago. She was over 110 years old. She couldn't talk English and never even tried to learn. She mainly stayed around people who spoke Comanche. Stella and Hilda went to go visit with her in a nursing home in Lawton not too long before she died and they had a heck of a time talking to her. She laughed at them 'cause they couldn't speak Comanche very good.

When I lived out there, every quarter of land had a house on it. Other Comanches like Uncle David—his last name was Powaway—lived the next quarter south of us, on the hill. We visited all the time back and forth. He got mustard-gassed in World War I and he was in bad shape when he got back. He had a government pension from the service because he was pretty well crippled. He could get around but had a hard time breathing if he did physical things. His wife was Evelyn, and her first husband's name was Pekah. Her son Levi Pekah was something else. He'd go down on the creek and play like he was Tarzan. You could hear him hollering down there. He'd climb around on those grapevines and yell. He rode a big spotted horse. His brain wasn't nothing but half a full deck.

Levi couldn't turn his head, he had to turn his whole body. He got him a motorcycle, and my brother who drank all the time, Roy, used to ride behind him. Since Levi couldn't turn his head, just his whole body, they had a wreck two or three times 'cause every time he turned his body he'd move my brother, who was sitting on the back. He's still got that place right south of me, and he willed it to his two daughters. I don't know what happened to him.

We used to play tag on the horses down on the creek at night. Liked to have killed us. We'd steal watermelons from a guy next to us who had good ones 'cause he grew them in sandy soil. One night me and J. T. Dobbins and Hoot Gann went to get watermelons on a farm that was two miles south of us. We had them melons tied on both sides of the saddles. We was coming back with our stolen melons and that farmer came after us in his Model A and we started running them horses with the watermelons swinging, and Hoot's horse tripped, fell, and the watermelons busted. Hoot got up with watermelon all over him and we took off.

Levi had one boy, I can't think of his name, he was about twelve, and he was riding a horse, going home, and he fell off the horse and his head hit a rock. He died at the Indian hospital. He was always over at our house. We had a wagon trail from their house to ours.

A lot of our neighbors were colored. One time this colored guy gave me a coon dog. I'd go hunting with him and trained him to catch possums and skunks. And then that colored guy came back to get him. He went to my Dad and told him he wanted his dog back—but he had given that dog to me. Dad never had a cross word for nobody, so he said, "If it's your dog, take him."

So I started throwing a fit and crying and didn't want him to do it. And then Dad said, "Where's the dog?"

I said, "He's tied up by the chicken house." And Dad went around to get him. And I got my .22 and loaded that bugger up and went around the other way. I met that colored guy and I said, "Now, you're not gonna take my dog."

And Dad told me, "You go put that gun back and don't you ever point it at anybody at any time." He took my dog. But he wouldn't have if Dad hadn't said that.

This one farmer down on the creek always came through our property. There was a gate about three hundred yards up the hill, but he'd cut the fence instead of going through the gate. Dad told him not to do that, and one time he come through there anyway and Dad watched him cut the fence. So Dad got the saddle on his old horse and went down there. Well, me and my buddy Ralph

Cocheta doubled up on his old sorrel and watched Dad. That other guy started to go through the cut fence so Dad took his lariat rope off his saddle and roped him, pulled him off that wagon, drug him a little ways, then stopped and went back down there and backed the wagon off our property. From then on, that guy always went through the gate. We couldn't hear what he was saying, but that white guy was really motioning with his hands. I'd like to have been there to hear what Dad said, but I know it wasn't cussing, 'cause Dad never cussed, smoked, or done anything like that.

Other folks, like some gypsies, came through one time for a couple of days in a covered wagon and camped east of the home place right on the creek. We were scared of them, so we didn't mess with them. I don't know if they were Romanian or what, but they camped down there in wagons.

★ ★ ★

Some of those old people helped to doctor us. If we ever got hurt we'd go to see them. There was one real old colored lady and she and her husband smoked a cob pipe. They were so old they couldn't do much, and everybody helped them. We went to see her when we got hurt, like when I almost cut my toe off with an axe. The first rattle out of the box I had to go down there to her, bleeding everywhere, and she used kerosene and sugar to make a paste, then put it on my foot and wrapped it up. Didn't burn or hurt. She was like a mother to all of us.

A lot of people had the whooping cough real bad. When any of us coughed we drank her kerosene mixture. When one of my sisters had whooping cough real bad, the old lady, she sent me and the colored buddies of mine out to look for a turtle, one of them land terrapins. We looked everywhere and finally found one. We took it back to the house—a shotgun kind of house where she lived—and she cut that turtle's head off and bled it into a coffee cup and mixed its blood with kerosene and a little turpentine and gave it to my sister. Then she wrapped her throat up and she got better. But I remember some of them people had it so bad, they coughed so hard they couldn't breathe. Just took their breath away and they died.

Lots of little kids died back then. Seemed they got sick and died. Not too many injuries. Lots of little kids are buried out at the Eschiti cemetery. My brothers and sisters died when they were young. No vaccinations, not good health care, either. Simple problems of today turned into something that killed them back then.

One time all of us were out chopping cotton and it was hot. Stella had a heatstroke. She just flopped over in the field. We ran over there and Dad knew what was wrong. Back then we'd get those old crock jars and put a bunch of wet tote sacks around them to keep them cool. Then they picked Stella up and set her under a tree and dumped the water on her. She came to and she stayed there a long time, and finally Dad got the wagon and took her to the house.

When I was young I was sick a lot. My sisters told me that when I was small I almost died. I had diarrhea so bad and they couldn't stop it. They didn't expect me to live, but one day I got better. Then when I was sixteen I had my appendix taken out. I had the appendicitis operation in the Indian hospital and I stayed in there a month. All the doctors and nurses were white people. For everything out on the farm, they give us caster oil. I had what seemed like a stomachache. So they gave me oil and that made my appendix bust and I had to stay in the Indian hospital for months, it seemed like. I had drain tubes stuck in my gut for along time. Stink, ga-damn. I got big scars too. Today when you have that surgery the scars are little. I got all kinds of scars on my stomach.

Before I was completely healed I went hunting one day with my new .22. I don't know why them dogs didn't go with me that day. I went over there toward the cemetery to hunt back in there, and along comes this bull. I knew he was in there, but he had been laying down in some trees and I couldn't see him. Well, here he comes and I couldn't get away from him. I was like from here to the road [about 150 feet]. I tried but I couldn't make it because I had just had my appendix out and was still real sore. He was gaining on me so I just stopped and shot him five times with my .22 and killed him. Belonged to Herbie Johnson. He wasn't mad about it.

I went home and told Dad, "I killed Herbie's bull up there."

And Dad says, "Why?"

And I said, "Because he was gonna get me."

And we all went over there across the creek from the house, and Dad went in there and talked to Herbie Johnson and he told Dad, "Well, you better go butcher him, then." And all them Indians come around then to help butcher and then to eat.

★ ★ ★

On the weekends we all went swimming or had a box supper. Girls would cook up something, like sandwiches and a pie, then the boys would bid so they could eat dinner with the girl they liked. Adults would pay for a box so they girls could have money for Christmas or something. All the neighbors came, either by wagon or on horse. All the colored people, the friends of ours, came over to our house at night, and we popped popcorn and roasted pecans and everybody'd sit around and talk, then we'd listen to the radio. We had one battery-operated radio, and everybody sat around that radio at night listening to westerns and the Grand Old Opry. We had a woodstove to keep us warm in the wintertime. Our car also had a little radio inside. One day Roy figured out a deal. He had a fan on the car and rigged it up to a generator and to the car battery. When the wind blew it turned the alternator and kept the battery charged up.

We'd go out in the fields and play, then we'd go swimming in a little pond about three feet deep, but at first I couldn't swim. I had to watch my brothers pretty close because they wanted to catch me and throw me in so I'd learn to swim. Back then I could run fast, but those colored boys could outrun me. I got to where I could dog paddle. Boy, I could get with it then. One day I was down there and they threw me in and I dog paddled right out of there, and after that they never bothered me again.

We had lots of boxing matches on the weekends. Them colored boys, Indians, white kids, everybody came over to box. Then afterward we'd play basketball in our barn. We had boxing gloves and a bag hanging in the barn. It was a big deal to play sports. At a certain time in the evening we had to quit to do our chores. We never went out to box at night because Dad thought we'd knock over a lantern and start a fire.

Me and my brothers and sisters didn't have any money, and at the little town called Stringtown there was a little store with a couple of gas pumps. The kind with glass on top so you could see the gas in it. Gas then was five cents a gallon or something. The store had an old-timey insulated box with ice in it, and that's where the pop was. Jimmy Eschiti would buy us strawberry soda pops and peanuts, and we'd put the nuts inside the soda pop. And a lot of time if we was going to the store and he was over there, well, he'd give us some extra money to buy candy. He was crippled from polio and had to sit in a wheelchair. He could drive by pressing the clutch, accelerator, and the brake all with one foot. He taught me to drive that old Buick. He'd loan me his old car to drive. I have to wonder what would have happened if we had money like they did from an oil lease. But all we did was farm.

* ★ *

Ralph Cocheta and me hunted and fished and played basketball. We went to school together, and he wouldn't talk English, he always talked Comanche. Me and him run around together on our horses and rode back and forth to our houses, he'd stay at the house or I'd go stay at his. He lived two miles south of us, and my family would go visit his a lot. His folks had peyote ceremonies down there. Ralph could sing peyote songs. You had to sing five peyote songs before you go and sit down in the peyote tent. We went in there and Ralph would sing for me. I'd go in there sometimes and watch those guys in there. Me and Ralph never did peyote. They were little bitty button things, and they'd chew on them or make tea out of it. Then they'd puke and feel better afterward. It made them kind of high; they'd feel good and say they talked to God. They would really sing, too. This guy'd sing, then that guy'd sing, you know, all the way around the circle. I could just hum a tune. They'd tell everybody in Comanche what they were gonna do.

One day we was down at Ralph's place and his stepdad was making medicine. I don't remember his name. He said he was a medicine man. This lady, she was sick and they had her in the back room on the bed. Me and Ralph knew he was there so we watched through the window. Ralph's stepdad had an eagle feather and was blowing on her and waving the feather across her body. He was mumbling something in Comanche and he just kept carrying on and on, then he started sucking on her stomach. He had a little bowl on the table, and all of a sudden spit out two little bugs in it, like the ones in ponds—water skimmers. He claimed he sucked them out of her body. He put on a pretty good show. That lady thought he cured her. I guess he did. She didn't come back no more. Maybe she wasn't that sick.

I think them medicine men are more like psychiatrists. The people who go see them believe in that medicine. If the sick person is patient and believes that the medicine man will cure them, then they will. It's up here in your brain. Mainly, it was the older people who believed in the medicine men. If I was in the hospital and was being treated by a white doctor, then I'd also let a medicine man come in and pray with me.

★ ★ ★

I went to the Beard School when I was about six. It wasn't too far away. I cut through the fields, and sometimes I brought my horse and would tie him to the fence and leave him a little feed. Had a cellar and a door on each end. If a tornado came up then everybody hit the cellar. We had a kerosene lantern for light. That's where I learned to read and write. It was just one room. Up in front it had a little place where the teacher stood. All the desks were lined up in neat rows. And there were kids of all ages there, some so little they fell through those big desks. Some of the grown men around there came to school along with the little bitty kids. We had to bring our own pencils and paper, and they supplied the books.

The teacher's name was Fern something. Her husband died and she married a guy named Dick Walker. She died about eight years ago—she was real old. I liked her a lot. It wasn't an easy job for her. All the kids were a different age, they came and went, and nobody was at the same level. A lot of those kids who acted up said, "That teacher won't whip me," but what she did was to get the bigger boys and they'd hold the one who misbehaved down and he'd get swatted. If she needed help, there was always some around for her. Kept us honest.

There were about as many Indian kids there as there were white kids. The teachers never really talked about Indians there. They treated everybody the same. My sister Stella would really get into it with some of the white kids who ran Indians down by talking bad about us, and she even got into some fistfights.

There was one boy who kept picking on me. I had a lard bucket that I carried my lunch around in. We took our own lunches every day. He wanted to give me a hard time so he jerked it out of my hands, then kicked it and bent it all up. Then he started pushing me around. Well, here came ten-year-old Stella, and she told him to leave me alone, and then he cussed her and she got the best of him in a fistfight. Stella popped him in the face and walked away. Man, they played rough back then.

Willard, a guy who became a good friend of mine, used to whip me all the time when we were kids. Man, I was scared of him. I used to run away from him and he couldn't catch me 'cause I could run fast. I ran all the time out there. I always run to Duncan and anywhere else I went. I tied down the top rows of the barbed wire so I could jump the fence, and when I got thirsty I'd get a drink from the creek. Wouldn't take me long to get anyplace. Well, Willard was mean back then, and sometimes he'd take the bridle off my horse Skeeter when she was tied to the fence and she'd go home without me.

He hit me pretty good sometimes and I'd just take off running. My brother Johnny told me one day that the next time he did that, "You fight him. 'Cause if you don't fight him, then he'll do that every day to you. He might whup you, but you fight him anyway. And if you don't, when we get home then I'm gonna give you a whupping."

Well, one day Willard kicked my lunch bucket and I took off running. He chased me and threw rocks at me and when Johnny heard about it, he got one of them check lines off the wagon team and I mean he busted me hard with that thing. I started crying and told Daddy about it and he told Johnny not to do that again.

The next day, Johnny said it again: "If he does anything to you, then you fight him. I know you can fight. I don't know why you let him do you that way." After two or three days, here Willard came again, and man, I busted him. From that day on, he never bothered me again. He was just bullying me around. He figured I was too much to deal with and he left me alone.

Those white kids only called us Indians bad names once or twice. After they found out we wouldn't take it, then they stopped. Back then, you could have a good fist fight and after the other guy'd had enough, they'd say so and you could become friends. Not like today, where you get sued or shot. I don't remember the white adults ever saying anything bad about Indians. They always referred to the colored people as "niggers," but they didn't mean anything bad by it. Some of my friends called me "Chief" or "Indian," but they're my friends and it doesn't bother me. But, if a stranger says it to me, then we'll have trouble because I know they mean to run Indians down.

Later I went to a school at Stringtown, just to play basketball. It wasn't close to my house. By road, it was about two miles, and I walked or ran. Went straight across the pasture, or took my horse and let him go, or tied him up and rode him home in the evenings. I came and went through eighth grade—I think. To be honest with you, I don't know if I got out of the sixth grade or not. There wasn't a requirement that we had to go. I liked it, though. I liked to play basketball, and we won some trophies. Played on regular old mud floors. There was a combination of white and Indian kids.

Stella went to Haskell to study nursing but had problems with her thyroid. Liked to have killed her. I remember my brother Johnny and Dad went to get her, and she stayed back at the house. We were all still there. It was in wintertime when they went to get her, and there weren't no heaters in the 1920 Model A Ford so they put candles on the dash and they blackened the windows.

After school I stayed around the house and farmed. I stopped going 'cause I lost interest in school and they needed me at home, both. I know it was my fault, and after I got older and smarter I wanted my kids to get the education that I didn't have. My dad always said an education is one thing people can't take away from you. I don't know how I got through the Marine Corps later on. I should have stayed in school. I really messed up.

★ ★ ★

Around 1938, Dad got sick and we quit farming and all the kids went everywhere to work. I stayed out there at the home place 'cause I didn't know how to do anything. When dad left, everybody left, and I was the only one left. Didn't know what to do. I lived out there by myself for three or four months. Stella, she got a job in town as a waitress. Sometimes I'd walk into town, or a lot of times catch a ride with farmers I knew. Stella'd buy me some lard or bread or I'd bake my own. Then I'd walk back home.

I didn't need no money to live out there. I just hung around. Didn't read anything. I got to thinking there were other things I could be doing. Stella kept me motivated, was always on me and looking out for me. Even though she wasn't making much working as a waitress she always gave me spending money, and when I walked to town Stella would give me food from the restaurant.

So while Dad stayed in Fort Worth with Stella and later with Hilda over in Lawton, I lived out on the home place and went hunting and fishing. I'd get a rabbit or squirrel or something for lunch or dinner, and usually I'd boil it. A lot of times a neighbor out there'd be farming and I'd get some roasting ears and bring it back home and boil it. I stayed out there by myself and rode my horse and never was sure what I'd do next.

After I'd been at the home place by myself for a while, Stella told me that I needed to find a job. And I said, "Well, I don't know what to do." I don't know how old I was then, maybe twenty. It was around 1943. The only thing I knew was farming.

Stella said, "You oughta find you some work here in town." A lady she was staying with was the manager of an apartment where Stella lived. "We'll find you some work," she said. Her name was Grace Gann, Hoot's mom.

Stella and Grace came out there in an old car and got me and said they got me a job. "You're gonna work for Halliburton," Grace said.[8] So I went up there and filled out an application and went to work, but had a heck of a time trying to get back to the house 'cause it was too far to walk every day.

Me and this friend of mine messed around at lunchtime. He had a Model T, and we'd ride up there to the café every day at noon and we'd watch them girls walk around. That's how I met my wife, Fern. I saw her and thought she was awful pretty. I'd watch her every day walking back and forth from Duncan High School. I was bashful and didn't know the first thing about anything like that. I used to shoot pool a lot, too. Fern and her cousin were always out looking for me. She said she wasn't but they were. Finally I got to talking to her, and we'd meet in town most days to talk and to go see a movie.

FERN

First time I ever saw him was at a basketball game at Duncan High. We didn't talk or anything. And then later we would see each other when I'd go to town to eat lunch during school and then go back by where he was eating lunch, ready to go back to work. Later we started speaking, and a time after that I was in the movie downtown and he came in and sat down by me. He told me his name was Charlie and that's what I always called him.

And then we started going out together to the shows. That's all there was to do in Duncan. We'd go to a preview—the late show at the Palace Theatre downtown. It was right across the street from the courthouse. The courthouse was like an island at the west end of Main Street. The building was surrounded by grass and a big retaining wall, and you could drive your car in a circle around that whole area. I'd visit my friend who was the daughter of the jailer, and we'd sit up on top of the courthouse looking across Duncan with our legs swinging over the edge. Charlie and I'd get home real late. Maybe sometimes during the week he'd come over to the house.

We didn't have a car all the time we got together. The only time we got in a car was with my cousin Wanda and her boyfriend Don Nelson. His dad had an old pickup, and sometimes Don would borrow that pickup and we all went out together in that.

A funny thing happened. My daddy worked at Halliburton and Charlie worked at Halliburton, and they didn't like each other at first 'cause they'd had words down there at work. Charlie told him, "Hand me that hammer," and Daddy said, "Get it yourself." And then Charlie came to the house to see me and there sat my daddy. It was kind of a funny situation.

We went out for a couple of years. I was fifteen. And then we got married when he came home from the Marine Corps boot camp.

People looked at us when we walked into public areas—an Indian man and a white woman, but we ignored them and went on. My family didn't say anything about it, but his family sure did say a lot about me. Only one time did someone in my family say something. Uncle Jim, who had a farm between Duncan and Velma. Well, everything happened in downtown Duncan. Either you were sitting in the streets or walking up and down the streets. One afternoon we were walking down the street and saw Uncle Jim and he said something prejudiced. He said, "Hello, blanket," to Charlie, meaning "blanket Indian." He thought he was cute, but it made me mad. I told him I'd never speak to him again if he was gonna act like that, and he never did it again. After that, Uncle Jim was nice to us. We all got along and I loved him very much.

My mom and dad were very nice people. When we went to get married my dad told him, "Charlie, all I ask of you is that you be good to Fern."

And Charlie said, "I will." That was all there was to that.

None of his family hardly liked me at all. They were mean to me, especially his sisters. Charlie's oldest sister, May, said that it was my fault that our first baby died from a birth defect. I never got over her saying it was my fault. Our baby died from spina bifida, which is caused by a deficiency of folic acid.

Charlie's dad was always good to me. I remember he always wore overalls and told us stories about animals and farming. He would always say that our kids would be something big one day. He had soft skin and a kind way about him.

So did May's husband, Jack Portillo. He was a full-blooded Mexican. The men were nice. His other brother, Roy, and Ned Timbo were nice, too. Hilda never was real nice. I guess they were jealous. What I always figured was that nobody was good enough for their baby brother.

We went to Wichita Falls and got married when he was on leave. I had my blood test, but he hadn't had one since he couldn't get away from the base, so we went to Wichita Falls where he didn't have to have one. Went on the bus. Stopped in Anadarko[9] and got his lease money at the Indian Office and bought me a ring. Twenty dollars. It just wore out; just wore clear in two. I had an engagement ring. He sent that to me in the mail from Arkansas in 1945.

Stella was married to a white man, Edward, almost as long as I've been married to Charlie. But I don't think he faced the same prejudice as me. I don't know why Stella married a white man. After telling Charlie not to marry a white woman, she married a white man. So did all of them women who told Charlie not to marry me.

Service as a Marine

The best times of Henry's life were when he served as a combat soldier in the years after World War II. Like many of the other twenty-five thousand Natives who took part in the war effort, Henry is well aware of the poor treatment of Natives by the United States government.[1] Yet our discussion of Tom Holm's 1992 essay "Patriots and Pawns: State Use of American Indians in the Military and the Process of Nativization in the U.S." revealed that Henry did not feel used or manipulated the way Holm describes other Native combat soldiers feeling while in the service. Henry enthusiastically enlisted in the service. Like most of the other Indians who enlisted, he had no intention of "becoming white" or of giving up his Comanche identity. He may have fought alongside non-Indians, but he had no expectation that racism and prejudice against Natives would suddenly halt by the end of the war.

Comanches, like the Navajos, Hopis, and members of other tribes, served as Code Talkers in World War II, and the Germans and Japanese were unable to decipher their language. Henry is perplexed and angry that the United States has not seen fit to honor the Comanche Code Talkers, although France honored them in 1989.[2]

Men whom Holm interviewed for his book *Strong Hearts, Wounded Souls* experienced emotional distress from their Vietnam experiences. In contrast, Henry talks about his military service very proudly and without emotional tension. Perhaps Henry did not suffer the same psychological problems as other Natives because of his confidence in himself, the pride he had for his tribe and family, and because his participation was an exercise in discipline and camaraderie that he craved, in addition to the opportunity to defend Comanches by defending the entity that has attempted to dominate his tribe: the United States. He did not encounter much racism, and any he did run into was dealt with quickly and decisively. Henry will not tolerate prejudice, nor will he fall victim to it. Indulging in a bit of ethnocentrism, however, Henry does believe that Natives have a better sense of direction than whites and that they are definitely better leaders.

Like the Native veterans of Vietnam Holm discusses in *Strong Hearts and Wounded Souls*, Henry does not believe that the individuals who made up the Communist or Axis powers were "all bad." He bemoans the treatment of the Japanese at the hands of U.S. soldiers and was especially distraught at the poor health conditions for children in China. At his home in Duncan, Oklahoma, Henry has numerous scrapbooks filled with photos he took during the war. A gruesome series of before, during, and after black-and-white pictures of the beheading of a Guam prisoner (that I must remember to remove before my young children take an interest in his scrapbooks) makes him comment, "He only did something wrong in the eyes of his enemies."

Holm writes that Natives fighting in Vietnam "tend to think of themselves as warriors of an older, sacred tradition, but placed in a changed set of circumstances."[3] Indeed, Henry's pride as a Marine and World War II–era veteran is the same sort of pride his grandfather Mihesuah felt while defending his tribe.

HENRY

I was still working for the Halliburton oil well cementing company when one day in 1944 this friend of mine said, "Let's go on a wheat harvest." It was common for young men to go on harvests to make extra money.

And I said "I don't know, I'm working. Can't just leave." Plus, I hadn't been on a wheat harvest before.

"Well, take off," he said. So I quit my job and we went to Garden City, Kansas, on a wheat harvest. From that wheat harvest we went all the way to Data, South Dakota. One day I got a letter from Stella saying I had to report back to Duncan because of the draft board. They had put me in 1-A for the draft when the war was going on and they were drafting me into the Army.

So, I came back home and there were about thirty to forty other young men going to Oklahoma City on buses to get physicals. Me and this other kid were talking, I don't remember his name, he was kinda heavy-set. I told him, "I don't want to go into the Army, I always wanted to go in the Marine Corps." From what I knew about it, I liked the Marine Corps. Every time I went to town and saw them posters of Marines, or if I saw them in the newspapers, I wanted to be one. My friends Hoot Gann and Lefty Gann had already signed up for the Marines when I had gone to work for Halliburton. My other buddy J. T. Dobbins also had wanted to, but he never did go into the service.

That fat boy said, "Too late now. We're in the Army."

Then I said, "No, it's not. When we go to Oklahoma City, we'll look for a recruiting station that's usually in a post office." So they took us to Oklahoma City and made us line up after we got off the bus.

We were walking around in a line and we got to a big building when the fat kid said, "There's the Marine Corps recruiting office."

Me and him just stepped out and went into the recruiting station and told the guy behind the desk we'd volunteer for the Marines. He accepted us and we took a physical. We went back to the motel to meet the others. They said they noticed we were missing and thought we just took off. The sergeant gave us a hard time about where we were. So the kid with me said, "We're Marines now."

The sergeant asked, "How ya'll getting back to Duncan?"

And I said, "On the bus."

So we went back to Duncan and after about three weeks—in November 1945—they sent us money for food and a ticket for the bus ride to San Diego boot camp, where we learned drilling and all that other stuff. After that, we went to Camp Pendleton, where I took my combat training. Got my clothes, got my head shaved, and was put into a platoon. Boot camp was tough. If you couldn't make the grade then you were out. Even those who tried real hard and couldn't make it were out, but at least they got an honorable discharge. Some people say training's not as tough now as when we went through it. I think women shouldn't go into combat. They claim that they can handle it, but I don't think so. In the Corps they teach us to take care of the guys next to you and you weren't afraid. If you died, there was always somebody there with you. And they'd get you out one way or the other. I doubt it if a woman could. I don't know. I don't think they could stay in combat conditions. Or maybe I'd just be worrying too much about them and if they really can fight. I don't know.

Anyway, we stayed in those aircraft hangars and slept on cots. We had all sorts of things to eat. No greasy stuff; it was good food. That was the first time I had really good food three times a day. We also got up at three, four in the morning when our sergeant came in and turned the light on. He had a swagger stick that was about two feet long. On the end of it he had a .50-caliber machine gun barrel, and he hit the metal trash can with it. I mean, he hit it hard and made all kinds of racket. We fell out of beds, hit the floor, got up, then fixed our beds right quick and went to the bathroom to wash up, brush our teeth and hair. It wasn't long before we were standing at attention at the end of our beds. Then we all fell out. We ran the parade field, which was a

1. Comanche horsemen Mihesuah (*left*), identified by his war shield, and Quanah Parker, 1899. *Photo Courtesy Robert J. Mallouf*

2. Joshua Mihesuah, Henry's father, in his early twenties (c. 1902), as a cowboy at the Burkburnett Ranch in Texas. *Courtesy Henry Mihesuah*

3. Henry Mihesuah in Eschiti's regalia, c. 1951. Eschiti was Henry's great uncle. *Courtesy Henry Mihesuah*

4. Henry Mihesuah in Eschiti's regalia, c. 1951. Henry hoped to purchase Eschiti's regalia, but relatives sold it to a museum before he had a chance to bid on it. *Courtesy Henry Mihesuah*

5. (*Above left*) Eschiti , c. 1900.
Courtesy Henry Mihesuah

6. (*Above right*) *Left to right*: Tuvette
with baby in her lap; Tuvette's brother,
holding baby; Tuvette's brother,
kneeling; Eschiti; unknown child, c.
1885. *Courtesy Henry Mihesuah*

7. (*Right*) Mumsuki and Tuvette,
Henry's mother's sister, c. 1930.
Courtesy Henry Mihesuah

8. Henry's mother, Carrie Peahbo, c. 1915. It is probably Martha in the cradleboard; Roy is standing in the lower foreground. *Courtesy Henry Mihesuah*

9. The home place, c. 1968. *Courtesy Henry Mihesuah*

10. The home place, 1999. Note how much foliage has appeared. *Photo by Devon A. Mihesuah*

11. (*Above left*) Henry and grandson Tanner Toshaway at the home place smokehouse, 1999. *Photo by Devon A. Mihesuah*

12. (*Above*) Henry and Skeeter, c. 1938. *Courtesy Henry Mihesuah*

13. (*Left*) Henry (*in front, right*) and his home place neighbors, c. 1930. *Courtesy Henry Mihesuah*

14. Aunt Tuseda, October 1971.
Courtesy Henry Mihesuah

15. Henry and Fern, c. 1946. *Courtesy Henry Mihesuah*

16. (*Above left*) Henry in China, c. 1946. The MP radio jeep is behind him. *Courtesy Henry Mihesuah*

17. (*Above*) Henry on leave at his in-laws, c. 1945. *Courtesy Henry Mihesuah*

18. (*Left*) Henry and his buddy Edwin H. Patrikis at Qinhuangdao, China, c. 1946. *Courtesy Henry Mihesuah*

19. Henry; his son, Joshua; and his father, Joshua, c. 1952. *Courtesy Henry Mihesuah*

20. Fern, Henry, and daughter Adele, c. 1950. *Courtesy Henry Mihesuah*

21. Adele and Joshua in powwow
clothes, c. 1962. *Courtesy Henry
Mihesuah*

22. Henry's best friend, Ron Halpin,
c. 1972. *Courtesy Henry Mihesuah*

23. Henry working on his bow, 1999.
Photo by Devon A. Mihesuah

24. Henry, 1999. *Photo by Devon A. Mihesuah*

25. Henry's brother, Roy, c. 1975. *Courtesy Henry Mihesuah*

26. Henry and Fern at their fiftieth
wedding anniversary, 1996.
Courtesy Henry Mihesuah

27. Henry and son Josh, 1990.
Courtesy Henry Mihesuah

28. *Left to right*: Adele, Fern,
and Joshua, 1992. *Courtesy
Henry Mihesuah*

mile. Then we rested a minute then fell out for chow. After that we did some more training with bayonets, or maybe with knives, where we learned the best way to kill a person. Then we'd box. After that we put on our full combat packs and went on a march through the sand. That sand marching was something else.

After chow one morning me and my buddy Patrikis put some new sheets on our army cots in the aircraft carrier. We left for a while and when we came back, those cots were all kicked over and the mattresses lay on the dirt floor. So I asked Elliott, "What in the hell happened here?"

Then he said, "God damn Gunny. He just started kicking cots over."

So I walked over to where Gunny was cooking eggs on his hot plate and I said, "Hey, Gunny, what's the idea of kicking our cots over?"

He turned around and looked right at me and said, "What are you, a spic?"

"Well, a spic's a Mexican, right?" And I said, "No, I'm an Indian."

Then he said, "Oh, you're one of them blanket-ass Indians."

I hit him in the face and his butt bounced off the floor. He swelled up a little. He was a smartass and I didn't give it second thought. I just knocked him down, so they restricted me for thirty days. See, you can't hit a noncommissioned officer. So they called the MPs in there to get me and then the CO came in there and he asked what was going on and I told him. And then I had to go see the Old Man, the Division Major or something. Anyway he was in charge of the Division. He asked me what happened and I told him. And then he said, "All right, I understand your side of it. He shouldn't have called you that. But you were in the wrong for hitting him. You're gonna be restricted for thirty days. In the barracks." But I never was. They never enforced it.

I never did mess up. Only one time did a DI [drill instructor] get on to me. We were doing marching drills and he hit me over the head with a swagger stick. We had on those pith helmets. It was hot and we sweated like crazy. He hit me on the head. WHAM.

"Henry," he said, "you're the only one in step." He meant I was the only one out of step. I thought the whole world fell in on me—hitting me in the head like that. I got into step real fast after that.

I also went to sniper training. I really didn't care about shooting somebody unless I had to, but I needed to be trained for it.

I thought about home all the time. Fern and I wrote letters back and forth while I was at boot camp.

What tore me up were those night compass marches. We were given compasses with luminous dials and a map, then we had to go through the woods to find what was left for us, like a canteen. I liked it because it was hard, it was special training, and I got to be alone. I probably liked it so much because I was alone during the day growing up at the home place. But I still knew I could rely on the other men in the Corps just like I could depend on my family.

There were a few other Indians I saw in the military—a Navajo named Yazzie, and Don, a Tohono O'Odham. The ones I knew about stuck together, although we were integrated. I mean we were all in there together. There weren't any black men in the Marine Corps. There was one colored guy in a construction battalion. But back then they didn't have any coloreds in the Marine Corps. As far as I know, Indians have always been in the Marines. Or they should have been.

In that compass march I did real well. I really do believe that Indians have a better sense of direction than white people. I also think the Indian leaders of long a time ago were more experienced in war than the any of the white leaders then and now, and they could set up an ambush better. There are a lot of Indians that are really smart and can outdo the white people, but there's also a lot who don't have any common horse sense.

I came home January 16, 1946, from boot camp for the first time. I wore my dress blues around, looking sharp, you know. Me and Fern got married across the Red River in Wichita Falls, Texas, after we drove down there on a bus. Just me, Fern, and a witness—some little old lady. That night we stayed in a hotel then went back to Duncan the next day to stay with her parents. Being married made it a little easier when I had to go back to war. I knew she'd be there for me when I got home. Boy, Fern didn't want me to go back, though. After we went here and there, visiting for about two weeks, then I went to South Pacific, to Guam. After that I went to Japan for occupation duty.

We went on a transport ship and took all our gear onto the dock. Then they put us on the amphibious ducks. First we went to an aircraft hangar in Nagasaki, then we went on guard duty at Hiroshima, where they dropped that bomb like at Nagasaki. I got a picture of where that bomb hit. They got a cross there, like from here to the gate [two hundred feet]. That bomb burned everything black and the trees were burned down to stumps, then it went right through the valley and up that hill. The other side was nice and green. There was a submarine base there where they built submarines, and the steel was twisted like a fire and a tornado hit it.

We collected guns in villages and put them on those barges and dumped them in the ocean. We didn't need the Japanese weapons so we just got rid of them. Every Japanese family got to keep one shotgun and five shells for protection. Outside of that, they didn't get anything else.

I had thoughts about what the United States had done to Indians and why I was fighting. I didn't think about it being the U.S. It's just a country and us Indians were here first. I was defending Comanches, yes, but also a way a life that Comanches and other Indians live. Which is mainly the white way. I also was defending the idea of democracy. Not everyone's equal in the U.S., but the idea is worth fighting for.

I needed to fight for our country 'cause I seen what the American boys did over there in Japan. If another foreign country took this one over, then they might act like the Americans did with the Japanese. They'd see a Japanese guy walking with his wife, and they'd take his wife away from him and that Japanese man would just bow. I didn't like that, but I knew that could happen here in the United States if another foreign country came over. I saw how the boys in war go wild.

And I saw them drinking too much. I was a military policeman and I seen them just walk up and knock those Japanese men down. I don't drink because my brother drank enough for both of us. Growing up and seeing other people drink, I didn't know why they did that. Why drink if it didn't make them any smarter, just dumber? They acted stupid.

And they'd give us those ration cards, like beer and whiskey and cigarettes—I didn't smoke—so I took my card anyway and I'd sell them. My buddies would go "slop shooting"—to a beer hall—and they'd drink beer and always get in trouble, and I'd be there with them. There had to be two MPs all the time in the slop-shoot. There were Marines, sailors, British Royal Marines. I couldn't leave them there drunk. We always had trouble like that. Especially with the other allies. The Navy especially, they'd give the Marines a hard time and we'd get in a fight. It was nothing for a Marine to kick a Navy guy's ass.

One Sunday morning after chow a gunner sergeant walked into the tent and said while he pointed at us, "You, you, you, you, and you. As of now you're military policeman."

We said we didn't want to be MPs because we didn't like MPs anyway. "Don't make any difference," he said, "you shoulda went to church. As of now, pack your gear and go to headquarters and you're gonna be an MP. Everybody has to requalify with a .45." So we went on patrol while the rest of the Second Marine Division was ready to go home. I wanted to go home too. I didn't have enough points, so they sent me and five other guys to China on the Red Draft, which was the same thing as saying we had to go on duty in China.

★ ★ ★

I was an MP in China with the last Marine outpost in North China. We landed in an APA transport, and since that was too big to go up the Yangtze River we got on an LST transport that could navigate shallow water, and we landed at a small place called Takubar. And from there we went inland on a railroad in a train that was like a cattle car. We all had on our combat gear—rifle, ammunition, sleeping bag, and a cot. We were going through that semi-desert country on the train laying on our sleeping bags and packs. And this other Marine was laying on his bag, and he looked out at that desert and said, "God damn. I don't know why we're over here. Hell, we oughta give it back to the Indians."

And I raised up and said, "Hey," and he looked up at me. "You apologize about the God damn shape it's in and we might take it back." And he scooted back down and didn't say any more but everybody kept razzing him about it.

They couldn't say my last name so they'd call me "Hey Indian." One time when we were on the bridges in China, the chief warrant officer called four of us over. He said to me, "Hey Chief, get over here." Then I yelled back, "What do you want, white man." Everybody got quiet then and that never happened again.

I didn't take nothing from nobody and they knew it. But what I didn't like was when we come back to America over there in California. I didn't like the way they treated Indians. They're always running Indians down in California. I had trouble with them taivos [whites] in California, but not in the service.

Me and my friend Marcasi took a jeep up on the Great Wall by putting chains on all the tires and driving it up to the top. That Wall was something. I wondered how the heck they built it. A lot of it was falling apart.

I thought Japan was dirty until we got into China. And that was something else. What I didn't like was those little Chinese kids with nothing to eat and their bellies sticking out. And every other day the Chinese came through there pulling weapons carriers—wagon-looking things. And they'd go around looking for dead people, and if a Chinese was laying there, they'd kick him or shake him, and if he didn't move they'd throw him in the wagon. Those people died everywhere it seemed.

There were a lot of train tracks, and we guarded all of them from Qinhuangdao to Peking. Sometimes there were three tracks in the same place, and Chinese people would run to cross one track but wouldn't hear the train coming from the other way and they'd get run over. Their bodies got all balled up and would lay there in the sun while the dogs pulled them apart. I remember the stench. They'd lay there until finally the army would come by with trailers and throw the parts in back. I still smell the decay of those bodies that were napalmed, or from grenades or firefights.

Them Chinese were fighting among themselves. Mao Zedong and Chiang

Kai-shek. Mao was a Communist and Kai-shek was a National. They'd fight between themselves, and we had firefights with them when they tried to take the bridges. I never saw Mao but I saw Chiang Kai-shek several times over there in Tientsin and Peking. He was a little bitty guy. I saw his wife, too.

We had to guard this one bridge. The towers that overlooked the bridge were made out of mud and straw and stood about nine feet tall. We used a stepladder to climb up. There also was a walkway inside where we could walk up when we did guard duty. During the day there was one sentry on the tower, while at night there were two guards. We had a field phone in there connected by a long line to the compound. We lived in Quonset huts. On the inside of those huts were sandbags all the way around. A lot of times, we'd be in there asleep or playing cards and we got fired on and bullets whined through the hut.

The sergeant told us that if we have a firefight at night, don't jump up. He said, "If you're on the cots, all you do is jerk your rifle off the cot and stay down 'cause those bullets'll go right through that metal. You get your weapon and crawl through the door and drop into the trench."

Then a flare would explode if it was at night. Anytime a firefight started, they shot flares and made it bright as daylight. And if Marines saw anybody out there, they got shot. Then we called the Chinese the next day to come get the bodies.

We were on a tower one night and got into a firefight with the Chinese. We could hear them walking up the tracks; you could hear them walking on that chat gravel for a long ways. So we challenged them and they got quiet then we could hear them messing around. One night we called up the command post on the field phone and we said that we challenged some Chinese on the track and they scattered and started shooting and we fired back. On each side of the track there was a slit trench that was sandbagged where we could get into it. We climbed down real fast and jumped into the trench since we'd rather be in the trenches than up on the bridge at night. We were safer inside them trenches. Our outfit shot off the flares so we could see everything. Nobody got hurt that night, but bullets were whining everywhere.

I remember one time I was up in the tower early in the morning and a Chinese train come by. It wasn't supposed to stop at the bridges but it did. It was pretty clear that the lieutenant in the Nationalist army was going to try and take over the bridges, and they didn't know what they were doing most of the time. So we couldn't allow them to take the bridges. Well, I said no, and tried to get them to move. I took my M-1 carbine off my shoulder but the Chinese had a Thompson submachine gun pointed up at me.

43

Anyway, I said to myself, "Hell, I'm in a mess here." So I laid my gun down, and wound up the field phone and told my outfit "I got a problem on Bridge 105."

Then Sarge cussed and said "Get them off that bridge."

I told them that I laid my rifle down and they had their Thompson subs on me. The guy I was talking to repeated that they'd be up there soon. So I took a hand grenade and pulled the pin out of it. I was thinking that I could throw it over to the train and duck in time, hopefully. It wasn't long before here comes this weapons carrier with a .50 cal machine gun mounted on it. It was coming up the track wide open and they couldn't stop and they were gonna hit the front of the train. One of our officers yelled at the Chinese to back off and they did. That's when the Chinese started talking good English. And then they started moving that train off the bridge. Then I had problems putting the pin back in the grenade. Marcasi came up there and he helped me put the pin back in. I really got scared that time.

Another time Patrikis came into where we were on bridge guard and said, "Henry, we found a Marine in there dead on the tower."

See, during the daytime there's just one Marine on the tower that was made of mud and straw, and they found him with his throat cut. What they think happened was a prostitute came up there and killed him. I knew that a Marine wasn't gonna let a Chinese come into that tower. We all figured a woman did it. She used one of them brush hooks like you use to cut grass with to cut his throat, then took his shoes, rifle, and ammunition.

It had to be a prostitute who killed him because any time a person started to walk up to the tower, the sentry would challenge him. We had wire strung across the field with trip wires and hand grenades hung on them. One night after I was on guard duty, I found some hands hanging on the wires. Just hands. I never knew what that was about.

We had four wires strung. The first was to warn anyone going across toward the tower. The next wire was a trip wire. If you hit that, then that's when everything went goodbye. One night there were two of us up on the tower, and I faced the track one way and my buddy faced the other way. It got real quiet and we listened. Someone hit the first trip wire and the flare went off. Then he ran and he hit the next one and pulled the pins out of the hand grenade and got blown up. Then we got down to see what it was. Turns out it was a big dog. Usually you could hear any steps on the tracks, but the dogs were quiet. It was one of them big dogs that herd sheep. It was a big white dog, not the Old English one, it was white. Lots of dogs also got shot 'cause they came into the dump and dug up trash we had buried. Some were wild, some were village dogs. Mules would get blown up too.

Villagers that lived not too far away from our compound had a habit of shooting right through our camp almost every night with tracers. But when they started, we took out our 37-millimeter cannon with a round a big as a salad plate and after we shot one round they'd stop until the next night. A Browning automatic rifle with a twenty-round clip worked just as well.

Once I guarded a lagoon. There was a bridge over it, and on the other end we had another guard sentry post. I was reading a funny papers book by an old coal lantern. It was about ten o'clock when I got through reading it. I laid it down and as I looked across the lagoon, I thought about how peaceful the night was. I didn't hear nothing. As I was watching the water, all of a sudden I heard a shot and the door splintered right by the side of my face. Man, you talk about turning the light out. Then I got on the field phone. All the Marines broke out then. They surrounded that lagoon, but they didn't find nobody. I don't know where that shot come from.

After that, Mao wanted to move our First Marine Division out of there. So the Chinese Fourth Armored Division come in to move us, and we wasn't gonna move, so we backed up against the beach and dug in to watch the three destroyers and one transport come into the bay. They had planned for the transport to take us off the beach. The Chinese destroyers looked like small dots way out on the water. When they shot, we heard the bullets whistling over our heads. And the whole ground shook. They fired about ten rounds and that was the end of it. They didn't take us like they thought they would.

Shortly afterward, we did train guard. Once, seven of us Marines went from Qinhuangdao to Tientsin. Normally it was about a three-day run and we took along our food and water. This time, it took us seven days. It took so long because the Chinese Communists were taking out sections of the track and we had to wait until they put in a new section of track so we could move. Since we ran out of food, we started charging the Chinese to cross the bridges, and we'd go over to the villages to buy food. Me and my buddy Golish sat up on the railroad car on top of sandbags with the sentries looking around through binoculars. He was built like you wouldn't believe; like a V and all muscle. Anyway, when one part of the track was finished, the next day we took off real slow and the Chinese shot at us. I looked across the fields and maybe half a mile away I saw an American flag flying. I couldn't believe it.

There was seven of us on train guard. Marcasi, Golish, Patrikis, and a few others hollered for the engineer to stop the train, but he couldn't hear us. I was carrying that carbine and went BLAM BLAM and when they looked back I told him to shut her down. I pointed to the American flag and then everybody could see it then. But like I always say, when I looked across there and saw that American flag, I just felt good because I knew there was help over there.

So I said, "I need some Marines to volunteer to go over to where the Americans are." Old Golish and this other guy from Tennessee said they'd go and they took off running. Then I said, "We'll give you four hours then if you're not back then we'll start looking for you. We'll be right here, we're not gonna move."

So they took off. And in a little while I couldn't see nothing except dust coming across the field. It was the Sixth Marines Detachment. They didn't even know we were on train guard. We didn't have any food and they brought us everything so we could get to Tientsin and then back to our detachment at Qinhuangdao.

Once we returned, we went on MP duty—patrol duty. We had radio jeeps and a big base unit. One Marine was always on the base 'cause we always had patrols out; usually two Marines were on patrol all the time. One radio operator and one driver.

Them Communists and Nationals were fighting all the time, and sometimes we'd get in between their firefights. We had a radio sitting right behind us on the jeep, and one night, me and Mark Hasey were on patrol and our CO told us that the Fourth Chinese Army was gonna move in there and bivouac the area, but they didn't know where they were. Well, off we went and didn't realize that the army had bivouacked in this one area we came up on, and they had sentries out. All of a sudden we'd see these Chinese guys with a rifle and they could see our headlights. So we stopped, and they motioned for us to come up to them and Marcasi said, "We better turn around," but it was too late because they were coming up on Marcasi's side of the jeep. There was a Thompson submachine gun between us inside the jeep—what you call a drum type—and we both carried .45s that we never took off. That bolt was always forward. When you pulled that bolt back, it was ready to fire. We also had M-1 carbines.

Anyway, one Chinese came running up on Marcasi's side and we both pulled out our .45s and Marcasi shot him. Almost point blank and blowed him backward. Them other Chinese fired at us and I called in and told them what Chinese unit it was and that we were being fired on by the Chinese. And that time the whole Marine crew came out. We gunned the jeep and took off down the road—them army jeeps are four-wheel drive and we were running probably forty miles an hour—but barbed wire was strung up across the road and we hit it. We got all tangled and since were going so fast we dragged it and kept on going.

Then we saw headlights coming toward us and we thought it was more Chinese. We were just barely going 'cause of that barbed wire wrapped around the axle so I grabbed the Thompson and bailed out on my side and Mark bailed out on his side. The headlights of our jeep were still on though. We got out of the lights so they couldn't see us, of course, then Marcasi crawled over to the jeep to hit the switch to turn them off and almost got tangled up in the wire. Then we heard people talking Chinese. At the same time, here came the Marines down there on their six-byers [two-and-a-half-ton trucks with six wheels]. We still had the radio and told them where we were and they said to flash the lights. It was dangerous to flash our lights 'cause it would have let the Chinese know where we were, but we had to tell the Marines where we were. They started firing behind us and we had a real firefight for a little bit. One Marine got wounded and I don't know how many Chinese got killed or hurt.

We always had lots of firefights with the Chinese. Now men get all kinds of ribbons and metals and stuff and we didn't get nothing like that. We did it because we had to. A lot of times in war I was scared, but really, I wasn't scared until it was all over. I was too busy trying to protect myself and the other men. I was in a rifle company and we were told what to do, what trench to protect, which machine gunners to help out. For a while after the war, I'd jump at loud noises and sometimes start shaking. Maybe it wasn't so bad for me because I used guns all my life and was used to the noise.

I always wondered why we didn't get anything for fighting like they do today. All I got was a pin called a "Ruptured Duck" that said "China Service." It's hanging in my house by the front door.

★   ★   ★

After my China duty in 1947 I came back with the First Marine Division to Camp Pendleton in California, where I was still an MP. Then I was a brig warden. Late at night I'd write Fern letters on an old typewriter with my two index fingers. Then I was a corporal and was assigned to go out and pick up prisoners in another state. It was called "prison chasing"—AWOL prisoners. We always went by train and picked up whoever we were supposed to, then brought the prisoner back to Camp Pendleton. "If a prisoner gets away then you're gonna serve his sentence," is what my bosses always said.

Lots of times on my prison chasing duty it was one on one; I always carried a rifle. Then I was put into criminal investigation and assigned to be a card-carrying investigator. I had a .38 with me all the time and did most of my work in San Diego down there on the Marine training depot. Then I heard of an opening in McAlester, Oklahoma, for guard duty. I thought, "Well, I'll ask for a transfer," so and me and my buddy Patrikis put in for one. He wanted to go back home to a shipyard in Philadelphia.

About three weeks later, Patrikis came walking in and said we got a transfer. And boy, I was happy because I thought I'd be closer to home and Fern. Still, I told him I didn't believe him, and we marched over to the bulletin board and sure enough, they transferred him to Philadelphia and me to 100 Harrison Street in San Francisco. I didn't like that. It was too late, though. My buddy Patrikis got his transfer and I haven't seen him since, but I sure would like to. I know he got married later in life. I should spend some money and have an investigator find him 'cause I lost his address.

So, I worked security in San Francisco and I had a crew of Marines under me. I also drove a fire truck in that Marine Corps supply depot. We never did leave that place except for one time when the fire department called for backup. And that's where I got my discharge. They also wanted me to ship over for three more years and go to school as a criminal investigator at Camp Lejeune, an FBI school. But I didn't have the knowledge or education to go there. If I had confidence in my writing skills, I probably would have gone.

Fern was pregnant while I was in Camp Pendleton and we had a baby in 1948. We named her Cynthia Lee after Fern's dad, Troy Lee. That was hard when Cynthia Lee was sick. I got emergency leave and stayed home with Fern for the five weeks that Cynthia Lee lived. We stayed with Fern's parents in Marlow and we went back and forth to the Duncan hospital to see the baby, and Fern's dad had to drive because we didn't have a car. She never left the hospital where she was born. After five weeks she died of spina bifida and I went back to San Francisco to work. All my friends out there supported me and that helped. She's buried in the Eschiti cemetery. There's a marker.

★   ★   ★

I feel a lot better about myself being in the Corps. It taught people something to go into the Corps. When I came out, I had a family I had to take care of. I went to school under the GI bill so I didn't have to get a job out of desperation. I bought me a ring afterward that has a ruby inset and it says "He who has a trade has an estate." I believe it, too. I wore that thing almost completely out.

Fern and I went to Fort Worth with my sister Stella and her husband Edward. We didn't have any kids then and they didn't have kids. They had a house and we split expenses. Fern worked and I went to school. Stella stayed home and kept house and Edward worked for the City of Fort Worth. Then Edward and I went to school where I learned diesel mechanics.

I went two years to a vo-tech; took straight diesel for two years. It was really hard on me 'cause I didn't have the education. I can read pretty good, but I couldn't cipher all the words out like you should. That was hard and Fern helped me a lot. When I went to school, I learned something. Most of the guys I worked with down there and went to school with, they were working down at the aircraft plant in Fort Worth in White Settlement. Some of them worked at night and during the day they went on the GI bill. All they did was go to school and collect their money. That's all. They didn't care if they learned anything or not. And they always gave me hard time, telling me to go somewhere else and make more money, but I told them I was going to school to learn a trade for the rest of my life. I got to have a trade and that's what I did. I stayed there for two years. But I had a heck of a time with some of them books.

The Marines prepared me for school. I knew I had to go into the service 'cause they were gonna draft me, but I picked the Marine Corps because I think it's the best service there is. Everyone looks up to Marines as proud. I think it would help most all the younger people. It helped me. I didn't know anything when I went into the Corps. The only thing I knew was farming, and the Marine Corps gave me confidence in myself. I didn't think of getting an education when I enlisted, but I sure did a little while after. Well, I'm proud to be a Marine and an Indian. I'm an Indian Marine. The tradition in the Marine Corps is we look out for each other and that's what we did. That's what I wanted to be. A Marine.

CHAPTER FOUR

Relocation

After World War II, conservative reformers, scholars, and politicians pushed for the assimilation of American Indians rather than allowing Indians to become culturally heterogeneous in the United States. Many white Americans argued that because Indians received economic support from the federal government, they were being treated with favoritism. Western states, especially, desired Indian lands and pressured the government to open those lands for sale. John Collier was replaced as Commissioner of Indian Affairs by Dillon S. Myer, who previously had been in charge of the Japanese internment camps. One of Myer's ideas after the war was to scatter Japanese Americans throughout the American population so they would not be congregated together. Myer and his allies supported this ideology in what would become part of the policy of Indian relocation.[1]

In an attempt to acculturate American Indians to the ways of mainstream society and to simultaneously acquire more Indian lands and the resources found on those lands, President Eisenhower appointed Glenn Emmons as commissioner of Indian affairs in 1952. Congress quickly passed House Concurrent Resolution 108—the Termination Resolution—which ended the federal government's trust relationship with tribes. The resolution also included an end to federal protection of tribes and an end to federal financial aid. The government then established the Voluntary Relocation Program for the purpose of moving Indians away from their tribes to large cities such as Tulsa, Dallas, and Los Angeles.

Termination and relocation proved to be disastrous policies for Indians who were not prepared to function within white society. Utes and Paiutes in Utah, for example, were cut off from social services managed by the Bureau of Indian Affairs.[2] Because they could not speak English, they could not secure jobs, and because they could not supply birth certificates, they were not eligible for state or county aid. The Menominees in Wisconsin went from enjoying economic success in the logging industry to suffering economic collapse. Many poor Indians across the country were forced to sell their allotments since they had no access to BIA services.[3]

Under the relocation program, many Indians had difficulty adjusting to life in mainstream society. Many lacked social skills and did not know how to speak English, fill out job applications, use a telephone, manage money, pay bills, or arrive at work on time. Many were homesick and faced racism on the job. The relocation program ended in the late 1950s; the policy of termination was enforced until the early 1960s, when the Kennedy administration realized that the policy was a disaster, but it stayed on the books until repealed by the House of Representatives in 1988.

After returning home from the service, Henry made the difficult decision to leave his homeland and move voluntarily from Oklahoma to California in the relocation program. Henry is well aware of U.S.–Indian relations, and although he believes the government owes a heavy debt to tribes, he takes a dim view of Indians who rely exclusively on government assistance. He did expect the relocation commission to get him started, but he had no intention of depending on anyone indefinitely, so he spent months finding jobs without assistance from the commission. He had a turbulent life as a relocatee in California, which included racism, insensitive bosses and coworkers, homesickness, and a shattering traffic accident that almost killed him.

HENRY
Around 1948 I started working for the highway department out of Duncan. After a while they wouldn't give me a raise or nothing. They wouldn't give me that nickel raise 'cause I was the low man on the pole even though I could work on everything from lawnmowers up to one of them v-8 cabs. So I went to talk to Leo Quales, my foreman, about it. I asked him why I had to keep going out into the field and not get a raise. Why couldn't he send somebody else out there on the road?

"I'm gonna be honest with you," he said. "Henry, the reason we like you out in the field is that you're a self-starter. If we sent these other guys they always call back to the shop every twenty or thirty minutes asking what am I supposed to do about this or that. And you don't do that. The only time you call is if one of them low-boys are down and you can't fix it. We don't worry about you 'cause you usually fix it."

Even so, everybody got a raise but me. I thought I should just work out of the shop, but they liked me in the field. I was looking out the back double doors one day and old Leo came out there and he said, "Henry, you got a long-lost look."

And I said, "Yeah, I'm getting ready to check it to you guys. Because you're not treating me right."

Then he said, "Let's so talk to Swede Osbourne (the division manager) to see if we can get that nickel raise."

We went over there and Osbourne said, "you're the low man on the pole and we can't give you the raise." Still, he didn't want me to work in the shop 'cause he thought I was such a good worker. It didn't make sense.

They had one of them old John Deere tractors with two wheels about the size of plates out in front, and it broke. Leo said, "Go on out there and weld it on your way out."

I said, "I can't weld it because that little welder doesn't put out enough heat to weld it." Leo argued with me and told me to do it even though I didn't want to and knew it wouldn't work. Well, I went out and done it and a few days later it was pulling one of those street sweepers and the driver was going along about ten miles an hour and the front end broke again. And that's what Swede brought up, saying I made a mistake. Even though I told him that I said I couldn't do it with that little welder, he said, "You made a mistake."

"Well," I said, "when your boss tells you to do something you go and do it." Then Swede said, "Henry, I never made a mistake in my life."

I looked at him and got mad. "And that's how them God damn lies get started," I told him. "There's not a man alive that didn't make a mistake," and I just walked out and went home and told Ma I was going to quit. We had just bought that little house over there on North 7th in Duncan.

So I went to the BIA office I had a little bit of lease money in an account over in the BIA office in Anadarko. So I went over there to get it out. They said they'd send me to California on that relocation deal. They said they'd get me a job, a place to live, and they'd send my family out there. Everything would be paid for.

I said I didn't want to be obligated to anybody. I had a trade and didn't want anyone to give me money. But they really talked me into going. I said I'd go on one condition, and that was I didn't want my family coming out there. I didn't want to be worrying about my wife and kids. I just needed to worry about finding a place to live. "After I'm situated then I'll send for them," I said. They agreed and we made a deal.

We had our kids when we were deciding to go on the relocation program. After Cynthia Lee, we had Martha Adele, named after Fern's mother. Then we had Joshua Kim, named after my father. We were disappointed every time we had a girl because there weren't any Mihesuahs, except for Roy Jr. And everybody else had girls. And we had two girls, and I was disappointed but we were real happy when Kim was born. Kim thinks that we spoiled Adele, though.

Both were born at the Indian hospital in Lawton. When Kim was born they didn't think he was gonna live. They couldn't get him to breathe. He turned blue. They two basins: one hot water and one cold water. And they'd dip him in one then the other. Fern kept saying, "What's wrong with him? What's wrong with him?" She was just laying there in the delivery room thinking, "We finally got a boy and he's not gonna live." But finally he got to crying.

The problem was, he was a large baby. Long legs, long arms. Eleven pounds, thirteen ounces. Fern had to have so much pain medication that I think it affected him. But she never had any trouble when either of the girls were born. It was fairly easy. But she was in labor thirteen or fourteen hours with him. He wasn't all that late, just by two days.

Then when he was about eleven months old, he was dying in the Lawton hospital. Fern just walked in and took him home. But he would have died if we left him there. Couldn't touch him, couldn't go in the room, couldn't hold him. And I know they weren't feeding him and taking care of him right. He was just getting weaker and weaker and weaker. He was so weak we could hardly hear him. Sounded like a little kitten. Fern's mama and daddy helped us a lot. Adele was healthy except her tonsils and adenoids had to be taken out.

Anyway, I put my tool box in the back end of my 1950 Ford and took off down old Highway 66. My old buddy Hoot Gann lived in Delano, California, and I got there in the evening and I called him up, but didn't tell him who I was us. He said "Where you at?" And I said I was at a little drive-in. So he said he'd come visit. I went out there and sat in my car waiting for him. Soon I saw someone driving through there real slow and I saw that it was old Hooter. I got out and hollered at him and he stopped.

We shook hands and I saw he had a gun in his front seat and I said "Hoot, what you got that gun in there for?"

And he said, "Well, you know I got in trouble in Oklahoma for robbing somebody and I didn't know it was you on the phone, and I thought you were one of them from Oklahoma coming to get me." He was a tough egg. He was with the first bunch of Marines who landed at Guadalcanal. He fought all through there and came back. When I was growing up on the home place, he lived right north of us, and his dad made moonshine. Me and Hoot stole his dad's six-shooter one night to go frog hunting when we were little kids. Hooter had a heart attack about thirty years ago.

I left after talking to him a while and almost never found my way across that Bay Bridge. I went from the Oakland side to San Francisco and was looking for the motel on Sansome Street, right off of Market Street. Finally, I found it. I went on in there and told them who I was and the guy said, "Oh yeah, we got your room." I think his name was Page.

I'd say there were about eighteen Indians in that lobby. From all over the country. Some from Oklahoma. One I knew was a Navajo. Another guy, Don, was a Tohono O'Odham. And there was some Pimas and some Walapais. They were talking, sitting on lawn chairs. Never did see any Indian women alone on the relocation deal.

That hotel guy said, "You're from Oklahoma," and this other guy comes walking up to me and introduced himself. His name was Jimmy Harris, a Sac and Fox from Stroud. He had short hair and a leg fused at the knee. He walked like Chester on *Gunsmoke*.

"There's some rooms back there," the hotel guy said.

And Jimmy said, "He can bunk in my room." Then he turned to me. "I don't want any of them drunk Indians in there." Of course, I found out later that Jimmy drank all the time and that's how he had that car wreck that ruined his leg.

We followed the guy and he showed us the bathroom, and it had about a 75-watt bulb. Then we went to our room and there was a little old bulb, maybe a 30-watt bulb, and we couldn't hardly see. Jimmy and I talked for a while and he asks, "Where you parked?"

I said, "Out on the street," and he told me we better go take a look 'cause they have tow-away zones, and if you're in one they'll take your car away. So turns out I was parked in the wrong place. He directed me where to park then we went back to the room and talked. Man, it was dark in there.

"Jimmy, I can't see nothing," I said.

And he said, "Well, every time the light goes out he just gives us the same kind of bulb."

"Let's go down to the rest room and get that bulb and put it in here," I said. So we did and it was pretty bright then. We decided to go to bed and I pulled the covers back, and looked under the pillow like I always do, and there were bedbugs running everywhere. I went back to the manager and told him. Boy, I was bitter.

The manager said, "I'll get someone in there to spray it right quick for you."

"No," I said. "They're all over."

Jimmy asked him, "How come you been telling me these bite marks are just sand fleas?"

★ ★ ★

Anyway, I got my suitcase outta the room and took off. Jimmy asked, "Where you going?"

"I don't know," I told him, "but I'll see you Monday. I'm gonna find me a hotel somewhere and then tomorrow I'll go to that relocation center."

Well, I finally found me a hotel and didn't go back to that first one. I found the relocation center the next day and they were five stories up. They said they had me a job, and they also said they'd do something about them bedbugs.

They sent me out on a job. One of them relocation ladies went with me to show me where it was at. It was White Motor Company, a big truck shop. She left after she showed me the place and I went in there to talk to the guy. After I filled out an application I asked him where I could put my tools. He just looked at me and said, "You don't need any tools."

Then I said, "What do you mean? I hired on as a mechanic."

Then he said, "All you God damn Indians off the reservation think you know everything." He opened the door and I saw Indians in the back, sweeping the floors and washing tools. "You sweep the floors and wash the tools like the rest of them."

I said, "I'm not sweeping the floors for nobody. I hired on as a mechanic."

Then he started cussing me and I told him again that I hired on as a first-class mechanic.

He asked me, "Are you a journeyman?" And I didn't know what that was.

When he said it was a first-class mechanic who can work on anything, I said, "Yes, I'm a journeyman."

But he said it again, "You don't need your tools," then I busted him and he bounced off the floor. I couldn't get a hold of him 'cause he took off. And I thought, well, they're gonna lock me up for sure now. So I went back to the relocation office and they had already called up there about me. Man, I was bitter, mad. They called me an agitator when I walked in.

"We got a call about you," says the relocation guy. "You're an agitator, you know that, don't you?"

I said, "I ain't no agitator. I don't know what you mean by that."

"Well, you went down there and started trouble right off the bat."

"I didn't start trouble. That white man down there started running Indians down and I don't stand for it, not one bit. I'm a skilled Indian, a skilled mechanic, and I can work on anything. And he told me I had to sweep the floors and he got to cussing me and I hit him and left."

"Well, we got you a place to live," he said. "At a motel."

I was still bitter and I said, "I'll tell you something. When I went to Anadarko to sign up for this, they said if I had any problems to let them know, to call. And that's what I'm gonna do. I got problems over here and I'm gonna tell them that you got those people over there with them bedbugs. Would you sleep in a room with bedbugs?"

That guy said, "Well, no, I wouldn't."

And I said, "Well, there you are."

So as I went back down there to that hotel where Jimmy was, I thought about how I had to get some kind of job. The relocation office mailed me money for room and board every now and then, but I needed to work so I wouldn't be dependent on anyone. As I was coming in through Oakland I pulled up to a light next to those old Key System buses. They were surging and my old pea brain said they got those 671 Jimmy diesels in them. I worked with them all the time. So I got me an idea.

Well, I saw Jimmy back at the hotel and he was laughing at something. "We already heard what happened over there," he said.

"You know how to get across to that Bay Area, over to Oakland?" I told him that when I was coming through Oakland I heard these GMC Jimmy diesels surging and I wanted to see if I could hire out over there.

So we took off. And we got to Oakland, finally. "So what you gonna do now," he asked.

Well, we needed to find a telephone directory so I could look up the office and then go from there. So we were driving around looking for a telephone when one of them buses shot by and Jimmy said, "Henry, I got a better idea. Get ahead of that Key System bus, wait 'til it comes by, and we'll ask the driver."

So we shot ahead of it and waited by the bus bench. We watched it stop at the block before us and then stood up, waiting. A lady came by and had a little Chihuahua with her on a leash and he was wandering around and came over to where Jimmy was. Every time Jimmy moved trying to get away from it, the dog moved with him. Then it lifted his leg and that lady said, "He won't bite you."

Then Jimmy said, "I'm not worried he'll bite me, I'm afraid he'll kick me." Boy, I never laughed so hard in my life.

Well, the bus got there and I asked the colored guy driver where the shop was. I told him I just got here looking for a job and wanted to fill out an application to work on them. He said to go back the way I came. "Keep going and you can't miss it." He didn't say how far. Boy, we went and went and finally Jimmy spotted it and I went in and filled out an application and talked to the superintendent. The next day they hired me and I went to work for the Key System bus line that ran buses all through San Francisco.

So I told Jimmy I had to find a place to live over on that side of the bridge so we drove around. He said there was a place he knew about by Lake Merritt that had room and board. So we went there and it was a pretty nice place. It was painted white with some bricks around it. There was a long hallway leading to the dining hall with big tables. There was another sitting room with windows so you could sit and look out and watch people. There were trees and flowers around it. The lake was a couple of blocks away, and some people fished there, but I never did. It was a busy area. So we got out and walked around and saw people sitting all over. I asked one guy for information and he sent me inside to talk to this big lady in there.

"I'd like some information," I told her. "I just got into town and need a place to stay. And my friend told me about this place."

"Yes, we got room and board," she says.

I forgot what it cost, but it wasn't very much. "You the manager?" I asked her. She was a big old gal. Real heavy-set and real nice.

She said, "Do I look like the manager?"

Then Jimmy said, "You sure do. You could probably whup everybody in here."

She laughed at him. "I can do that too."

But old Jim, like I say, he was one of those guys. Well, I told her what I ran into over in San Francisco and asked her, "Is there any chance of getting those Indians out from that place and over here?"

"Well, we used to have Indians over here but they were too rowdy," she said. "We try to keep this place quiet and we get people every now and then drinking, but they don't stay very long 'cause we get them out."

"We got people over there that need to be somewhere other than where they're at," I told her. "Is there any way we can work out a deal? There's sixteen, all men without their families. I want to sign up to live here, but if we can come up with something to get them boys over here, you may get extra money coming in 'cause they're here through that BIA relocation program. They pay you direct."

So we sat there with her while she thought about it, then she says, "Well, on one condition. That you talk to them and explain to them that we don't want drinking or fighting or anything. You think you can control them?"

I said, "Well, I don't know. I can keep them from drinking here. They may be drinking out there someplace else. But if you're paid directly for their room and board and the relocation place doesn't pay them, then they won't have money to go booze it up." Course Jimmy was standing there and he boozed it up all the time.

Then she said, "I got to talk to someone else. How can I get a hold of you?"

I said, "Well, I'm gonna stay here."

"Oh," like she forgot. "Well, okay."

"I got a job working for Key System."

Then she said, "Let me talk to you after a while." So she got me a room and I got my suitcase.

I told Jimmy I wanted him to move over here with me.

We could pay either by the week or the month. I said, "I'll try it for a week." I went ahead and paid her 'cause I had a little money with me.

Then that lady said, "We'll take a chance with you. You said you'll run roughshod over them boys so we'll take a chance."

I went up to the relocation office and told Page where I was gonna be. And he said, "Well, I don't know how we can rig that up."

I said, "Well, I don't know how you will either, but I ain't living down there back at that hotel with bugs. I'll just call the BIA office there at Anadarko."

Well, Page said, "Henry, here we go again. I don't understand. We got you a job."

Then I said, "I already forgot about that job. Just like I told you before, I don't like people to run down Indians. That guy's probably been talking to them other Indians like that for a while and they don't say nothing to him. If they're not skilled, then they don't have another way to get a job, so they don't say anything and do what he tells them."

Well to make a long story short, twelve Indians came to the new place. The rest wanted to stay at that bug hotel. I don't know why. So I talked to them about drinking, that it's a nice place and no drinking or fighting's allowed.

And it was a nice place. I enjoyed living over there. It had a big basement, and someone was always cooking down there. When hunting season rolled around and I asked the lady what I'd been wondering about. "If I go hunting and kill a deer, will you cook it up for us?"

That big lady said, "You just bring him down here and we'll fix him." That heavy-set gal, you talk about playing ball.

"Well, I'm gonna skin him out and everything." And she said they had a cooler down here and I could put him in that.

So I went hunting with the guys from Key System. They were all Mexicans. One was an assistant boss, Joe, and the rest of the men were his crew. They insisted I go with them. Now, I do not hunt with people I don't know and I really didn't know them. I just worked with them.

I said wanted to take my own car, but that boss said I should ride with them.

So I lied and said, "Well, I may run around. I might want to go to some of them bars."

"Well, then somebody'll ride with you."

"No," I said. "I go by myself. I can sleep in the back of my car."

So we went on up there to hunt and sure enough, as soon as camp got set up they started drinking and shooting their rifles in camp and hollering. So I told old Joe something like, "I'm gonna go down to that bar and drink a little bit and wander around, see what's down there," just to get away from them. So he said okay and when I got in my car and didn't go down there. I went on dirt roads back in the woods to find a place where I could spend the night. I crawled in the back of my Ford and went to sleep.

It was barely breaking daylight and I got out. I looked around and decided to go up higher and I drove up to a rock formation and parked. Then I got up on those rocks and sat down and I could see quite a ways down. I just sat up there and I didn't know at that time it was called Monkey Rock. I was up there for about two hours waiting and listening to them shooting way down below me. Then I heard some rocks fall below me and I couldn't see what it was, then I saw a buck running with some does and I shot him and gutted him out.

I had asked that big lady at the motel if she had anything I could wrap a deer in and she had given me a soft rug, it was the only thing she had back there. So what I done, I skinned him and cut his head off and all I had was meat and the head 'cause I gotta have that durn head to put my deer tag on it. I left the hide where I shot him. So I drove straight back to Oakland and went inside the motel and that lady said, "Thought you went hunting."

And I said, "I did, I got my deer right here."

"You're kidding."

And I said, "No, I'm not. I just got back. Where do you want me to put it? I got it in the back seat of my car wrapped up. I don't want to get blood and stuff on the seat." The meat had fuzz all over it from that rug.

Old Jimmy says, "Boy we got soup now." He always talked about eating dog soup, too. Anyway, we took the deer down there and the lady cut him up. Man, she got after that deer like you wouldn't believe.

On Monday morning I went back to work and old Joe got all over me. We liked to have a fight 'cause I left to go hunting and didn't come back. He said that the reason I left was because of "us Mexicans."

Then I said, "I'll tell you the honest truth, Joe. Whenever ya'll were up there and you started drinking and shooting them rifles around camp, I decided to leave. I don't drink and I know you're gonna have trouble mixing booze and guns. Next thing you guys know you guys would grab a hold of me and make me drink. Just pour it down me." They tried to do that to me in the service, but I had too many buddies. And I saw them do it to other men and they'd pour it all over them trying to get it in their mouth.

Anyway, me and him got into it and he was mad. "I should just whup your ass," he said.

Then I said, "Well, if you're gonna whup my ass we better go out in that parking lot then."

He changed the subject and after that we got along pretty good. I found that people who talk tough like that, like they're gonna beat you up, back down when you hold your ground.

Me and them other Indians stayed at the rooming house hotel about three months, and finally Fern and the kids came out after I saved up some money. I found us a place, and Fern was happy with the little upstairs, one-bedroom apartment. Kim and Adele slept together. They came out on a train and we lived in an apartment in East Oakland that I got before they got out there. Fern can tell you a lot about it. The first year was pretty tough. Like in Oklahoma, we were barely getting along even though we didn't need much. I guess if I had called up the relocation office they may have sent me money. I don't know. Then things were pretty good after I could afford to buy things.

FERN

In September 1956, we moved to California through the relocation program. Adele was five and Kim was four. We were hardly surviving. Charlie didn't make much money. Only about two hundred dollars a month. Of course, things were cheaper then, but sometimes I didn't have enough money to buy milk for the kids and they both had bottles. That relocation program only got us started, it didn't continue to give us any money. Neither did the tribe. The program paid for us to get there on the train, and Charlie found us an apartment in Oakland. That's about all they did.

We stayed there almost twenty years. It got better. We had money to spend and could buy food and clothes. We lived in that apartment for three years with one bedroom for four of us. Kim had a cot in the bedroom and Adele slept on the couch. Then we moved to El Sobrante.

We didn't have any toys, so Kim rode the suitcases like they were horses. I just went out there on the train and only took clothes, nothing to play with. The first time we went back home I packed up the toys and books I had stored in the attic. We had rented our house in Duncan that we bought from a contractor friend, and our renters turned out to be a disaster. They never paid the rent, and they took my things and sold them and I had to look for my furniture then buy it back. For a long time Kim's footprints were in the driveway. We put them there when we had to redo the driveway. Charlie picked Kim up and put his feet in it while it was wet. Later, the federal inspector had the next owners tear up the concrete so the water wouldn't run in the garage. One time several years ago I went up there and talked to the lady who lives there but couldn't find the prints. Must have been cemented over.

We found out about that Intertribal Friendship House in Oakland, and the kids started going over there a lot. There weren't any other Indians around where we lived, but we found some at the Indian center. Kim and Del [Adele] would Indian dance, although Kim couldn't really dance. He was like a big old horse. He didn't have rhythm. But Del, boy, she sure could. One Navajo out there, his name was Jackson, danced with Del, and those two could really two-step together. I got pictures of Kim. It was a lot of fun.

We'd go to all the dances. They'd get invitations to go. My kids were on TV a couple of times. They got their outfits from the ladies' club at the Friendship House. I think we still have them. We paid for the material. A Comanche guy out there, Jim Wahnee, also taught them how to dance.

I took my kids to enroll in school and they asked me if I was the baby-sitter. That made me mad. I said, "No, I'm their mother." I kind of resented it. They were with me and they were my kids and those people could tell that I was their mother if they had two cents' worth of brains.

When Kim was a little boy we told him he was half-Indian, and somebody asked him one time which half was Indian and he said, "From the waist down." He had a white head, I guess. I don't remember him asking much when he was little. But he didn't ask much of me. I never taught them that they weren't Indian. I always told them that they were half. I never said anything mean about Indians, they just didn't understand what it meant to be half-blood.

When they took vacations in the summer they went to Oklahoma and stayed with my folks. The topic just never came up much. They knew they were Indians, but when Kim got in college he really became an Indian.

HENRY

We had friends come to the house a lot and they was Sac and Fox, and old Gene Harris, who was Jimmy's brother. Another friend of ours was Tohono O'Odham, Don Osif.

Jimmy was still there at that rooming house and was always in and out of everything, like jail. He stayed with us a lot when we lived in Oakland and sometimes babysat. Jimmy and Gene moved back to Oklahoma later. His girlfriend killed him about ten years ago at the Thunderbird Resort in the Choctaw Nation. They'd both been drinking, and after an argument she shot him.

I knew his brother, Gene, too. I sold that Model 50 Ford to him. He married a white lady who had a son and daughter and he raised them like they were his. That boy eventually joined the National Guard. Well, I later saw Gene when he moved back to Cushing, Oklahoma, and he had one leg amputated from diabetes. He traveled back and forth to California and went to powwows. Next time I saw him, his other leg was gone. Finally, Gene's cousin or someone wrote me and said he passed away.

Another guy we knew out there, Bob Duncan, had an old Indian skull he found in one of the Indian mounds back in the late 1960s. There were a lot of the mounds outside of Woodland. And when the farmers bought the land they bulldozed over them and that's where I found lots of arrowheads. There were lots of human bones, like knuckles and things. Lots of people went through there carrying things off. Well, Bob found a skull and its mouth was full of obsidian chips. Once he put a fake mustache, an old German helmet, and other stuff on it. He was always kidding around with it. Adele told him to take that skull back where he got it and bury it, otherwise something would happen. Sure enough, a few years later his house burned down and destroyed everything. He never admitted that was why his house burned, but he should have.

We lived in Oakland three years then we moved to El Sobrante because I was working for Union Oil Company in Rodeo just up the road a little ways. And after we lived there a little while I joined an archery club, in about 1959. And that's where I met my best buddy, Ron Halpin, in the early sixties. Nobody would mess around with him. If you didn't know Ron, you'd think he was stuck up 'cause he wouldn't say nothing to you. That's why I latched on to him. We started talking and hunting together. He'd been hunting a long time with a bow, but never killed a deer. So we'd go out and finally he killed one. We were best friends 'til he died three years ago.

I worked for the Key Systems for about six months, then they laid me off. But my supervisor said, "Henry, we're gonna have you back here working, 'cause we need you. I'll have you back here working in a week."

I said okay and went home and told Ma.

Then she said, "Let's go home."

We wanted to go back every chance we got, so in 1957 we packed them kids up and took off to Oklahoma and messed around there and then went back to Oakland because Fern had a job at the credit bureau. Got back up there and talked to my supervisor and he said they still didn't have anything open yet. He also said "Give it more time." So I thought, well, I'll try to work for a construction company with operating engineers that had a union.

So I went out there to talk to them and the head guy said, "It'll cost you $250 to join the Union of Operating Engineers."

And I said, "I don't have any money to join it. If I go to work, then I'll pay you."

He said okay and signed me up. And then he said, "Come to the union hall every day," and I did for while. There were all these guys standing around talking. Smoking and everything. I stayed there almost a week and nothing happened. So I asked them one last time if there were any jobs. And there weren't any. So I went to find me one.

I was out driving one day and found me a job working for Union Oil Company. Then they gave me a letter to take back to the Operating Engineers Union and God damn, those union people came unglued. They got right on the phone and chewed the Oil guy out, and then told me, "You see all these people sitting here? They were here a long time before you were. You don't go out and find a job before them." But as far as I could see, all those men were just sitting there.

He got talking smart to me and I just left 'cause I didn't want to get loud. Then I went to the Union Oil and explained and that supervisor said, "Don't worry about it, Henry. Them people up there, they don't want to work. They're just sitting up there on that bench, and if they did come to work, they wouldn't do nothing. I know them. I hired out of that shop up there. They won't do nothing."

Then the Operating Engineers Union said no again, I couldn't have that job, but I never had paid them 'cause I didn't have money. So I just forgot about it.

I got that job through Truman Wright. I knew him and his brother B. G. when I was a kid and we went to school together. He was an operator and he operated them big, heavy cranes two hundred, a hundred feet up in the air. He'd sit up on top of them durn things. I worked for them for a couple of months and then me and four welders got laid off.

Then my boss said, "I don't want you to go anywheres else, 'cause I'll have you back on the job in the week."

I said okay again and me and Ma and the kids came back to Oklahoma in the summer of 1959. Seemed like every chance we got we went back home. We didn't have any money to stop in hotels so we drove straight through on Route 66. When we came out of San Francisco, we hit 99 then 58 from Bakersfield to Barstow, then 40, which was 66. It was just a little highway. We had a new car by that time, and we tried to get station wagons all the time so the kids could play in the back and when they got tired they could go to sleep. Sometimes we stopped alongside the road to sleep. We didn't wear seat belts back then.

Then when we came back to California that summer, I went to pick up my coveralls at the shop and asked about jobs again and was told they didn't have any yet. I had heard about the dam they were building up at Lodi, and they got lots of heavy equipment up there. So I checked them out, and in the meantime I went back to San Francisco and filled out an application as a heavy-duty mechanic.

And the mechanic boss said, "We can give you a letter, but it won't do you any good. It's all union. The union's strong in California." I told them I had a problem with the union. Then he said, "What we'll do is send you to Saudi Arabia for eighteen months and man, you talk about the scale they have."

I said, "Well, I got a family here and I don't want to leave them."

Then he said, "We'll send your family back to Oklahoma and you to Saudi Arabia. You stay eighteen months you'll almost be a millionaire 'cause they send that money where you want it sent and you don't pay no taxes on that money."

I thought about that, but had already been overseas and didn't want to go back. Anyway, Gene Mayo from Union Oil Company called me and said that Carl called him and said I was a good mechanic, a good hand, and knew everything that he needed. He told me that if I wanted to work to come on down to Berkeley and fill out an application for Union Oil. The supervisor, Gene, said, "Henry, I don't know what kind of work you do, but we'll start you out as third-class mechanic and in two months' time, depending on how you're doing, you can move up like the rest of the crew."

I thought about that a little bit and agreed. So I went up there and worked for them and finally three months rolled by and I said, "Gene, my paycheck doesn't have a raise or nothing." Then he promised to check into it, and the next weeks rolled by and nothing happened and I told a friend that it didn't look like I was gonna get my raise. And then I asked him to load my toolbox 'cause I was gonna look for another job.

Gene overheard and said, "Wait a minute." Then he talked to a supervisor and he said, "You ain't going nowhere yet."

About an hour later Gene came in there and said, "Henry, here it is, you get your raise and all the back pay. It was gonna happen, you know."

But I reminded him that the money never showed up until I pressed it. I worked for them for over ten years. I was called a "Vacationer" in Fresno, Reno, and Sacramento. I had to go up and relieve the workers who were on vacation. I enjoyed being in different places. I got to meet a lot of people and got along with most of them. I made friends with one, who became a buddy of mine, Frank Montgomery. He lives down there at Ajo in Arizona outside of Tucson.

One day my boss came in and said they wanted me to replace Frank over in San Francisco.

I asked, "Replace him? You know, he's a good friend of mine and I'd rather you send someone else." But they wanted me over there.

They wanted Frank to work by them as assistant boss because he couldn't get along with those truck divers, and besides, all the trucks were broke down and they wanted me to take care of them. Well, less than a year later Frank quit and stayed in San Francisco. Then I was on call twenty-four hours a day. I had eleven trucks under me. Up to eight-thousand-gallon tankers.

I never thought about them giving me a hard time with my jobs because I was Indian, although it could have been. There was the black guy who worked there too. He was a real smart aleck and gave all the Indians a hard time by talking about how the white people whipped us. One time several of us went up north to hunt and he saw us practicing with our bows. He turned to me and said, "You Indians can't shoot an arrow straight."

Then I said, "I can shoot an arrow farther than you can chuck your spear."

Then he got mad and we almost got into right there. Everyone else thought it was funny since he was always mouthing off. Most of the people I worked with were easy to get along with, but the people I worked for—as long as they could make some kind of advancement because of me, or save the companies money, they would.

FERN

One day, May 29, 1969, Charlie was coming home from work, and on the Bay Bridge a Chinese kid came across three lanes of traffic and jumped the divider. Charlie was in the center lane and got hit head on. Killed that kid instantly. They said he was all doped up. Just a nineteen-year-old boy.

I got called about a car wreck, and when I found out I ran out the door even though I didn't know where I was going. Kim pulled me back into the house. He called Ron Halpin and he came over and got us, then took us over to the hospital. Charlie was in the county hospital because they didn't know him or where else to take him. It was nighttime, close to midnight. When I got there I had him moved over to the Merritt hospital, the better hospital over in Oakland. I don't believe he would have lived if we hadn't taken him there because they weren't doing anything at the county hospital. He'd just been laying there for several hours and they'd weren't doing nothing. Ron stayed at the hospital with us all night.

He was there nine weeks. Intensive care five weeks and not expected to live. Part of the time he was on a ventilator and then they moved him out into a semiprivate room, and he was in there a month. His chest was crushed and his leg was crushed and he had a head injury, but that cleared up pretty fast after they sewed it up. No seat belts on those Union Oil Company trucks. That was just about the time they were starting to put them in. That truck was only about one or two years old.

He had ruptures in his chest. He had two or three surgeries to reconnect everything that busted loose. And he had hernias. His leg grew back crooked and they had to go back and fix it a couple of times, rebreak it and straighten it. He lost so much weight his leg moved around in the cast. The cast didn't do any good after he lost weight. He also contracted hepatitis in the hospital from the transfusions and was quarantined for a while from that. He was real, real sick from that.

I was working at Berkeley and I took off work while he was so bad. And I'd drive to the hospital in Oakland every day on that Nimitz Freeway from El Sobrante, where we lived, north of Richmond. It was really, really bad traffic. It was scary but I did it. I'd go to the hospital and sit in a little waiting room they had outside of ICU and wait for the doctors to come by. He had several doctors and an orthopedic surgeon, Dr. Auerback. He would always tell me the bad things. Some would be nicer about it and tell me nice things. Henry had some real positive doctors who would tell us things to make us feel better. But this orthopedic surgeon, he just told us like it was, you know. And of course that always made us feel worse.

Ron Halpin stayed around a lot and help him. They wouldn't let anyone but immediate family in to see Charlie, so Ron told them he was our lawyer, and he brought a briefcase with him and went in all the time.

I was so upset and busy and everything myself I didn't have much time to think about how the kids were taking it. It was an ordeal that lasted for years. It's still going on 'cause his leg is still bad. He wears a brace on it. Kim was at home and Adele was away at school at the Institute for American Indian Art in Santa Fe. And I had a friend of ours call out there to Adele's school and they sent her home. She came home and never did go back. I went back to work and she stayed home all the time with her daddy. Later on Adele went to school at the Armstrong Business College in Berkeley. She got her degree from Armstrong College in Berkeley as a legal secretary.

After the accident the company he worked for took care of him for a year.

We paid for half the bill and the Comanche tribe paid the other half. And then they fired him—laid him off so they didn't have to worry about a suit being filed after a year. Statute of limitations. We couldn't make it out there on what we were getting. And so we got a lawyer and it took a long time to settle with the company.

HENRY

I had a twenty-pound sandbag on my chest. Every time I coughed I felt something move in there. My ribs were crushed, punctured my lung. Had to cut a hole in my neck so I could breathe. Then they'd go in there and suck that mucus out every three hours. Didn't feel too hot. And then my arm. The muscle popped loose at the elbow and they were gonna cut up here and reattach it. But I talked myself out of it. My leg just had an ace bandage around it. That surgeon said it was like a wet dishrag. On the side of my head, I still got a groove in there.

They didn't have painkillers like they do now, they just had shots of morphine, and I got to where I required it. Man, you get a shot of that and just relax and everything's just fine. No pain, nothing. They got me off it somehow. I was in the ICU. There was two girls who sat with me, and I couldn't talk, and they fixed me up with a bell so all I had to do was move my hand. And any time I breathed a little different, they were there quick as a wink to clear the tubes in my throat. Then I got pneumonia.

The guys I worked with and hunted with came to visit me. One was Wayne Polk. He sat down and we talked but I could just talk a little bit. He said, "Henry, I've been praying for you to get out of here." They called a priest in there and he wanted to give me the last rites and I said I didn't need them but told him I'd pray. Then I started thinking about them kids. Nobody to raise them. I wasn't about to give up.

One guy, his name was Edward. He was a doctor and had a cabin up there in Idaho and he stayed up there a lot. He said "When you get out of this we'll go up there to hunt. You're gonna get out of this."

This other doctor, he was a blood specialist. He told me, "You don't take no blood from anybody. Anybody tries to give you blood, you call me." One time, this Chinese doctor tried to give me some blood, and when I asked about it, he said it was orders from this other doctor. I told him I didn't want it.

Stella and Edward were the only ones in my family who came out. They drove all the way out there. Stella stayed with me when Edward had to go back to work. Whenever you need help, you can depend on them.

Well, I believe that I made it because I was in good physical shape. One doctor said that we're so advanced with all these machines, that's why I made it. I said "Yes, but the Lord had something to do with it."

FERN

It wasn't easy after the accident. He came home from the hospital with a cast on and crutches. He lost a lot of weight. He couldn't do anything around the house. It was sad. I did what I knew how to do. In February 1973 we moved back to Oklahoma. It was bad, you know. Somebody that was so active and did everything. Hunting, fishing, working, everything. It just stopped overnight. He wasn't able to do anything. We hoped we could make it on what money we had and Adele's income. And this lawyer kept fighting for us and he finally won a workman's comp case in 1975. We had insurance, but it didn't pay anything. The insurance company told us one thing, then another, and we believed anything they told us. We didn't have sense enough to go fight it.

Charlie's niece Eva was a Comanche Health Representative—CHR—she used to come check on him. I was telling her one time about how depressed he was and she made him an appointment with a psychiatrist at the Indian hospital. We didn't think Charlie'd go, but we talked him into it and he did. And he saw him for several years once a week and it helped him a lot.

I never thought anything would ever happen to him. People told me how close to death he was, but I never, ever thought he'd die. Everybody thought he wouldn't make it. But he did.

He hasn't worked since the accident. We went to court to win it and was a lump settlement. Lifetime medical on his leg and a lifetime pension we can draw on. He also had a payroll protection plan through the Union Oil Company. That was the biggest mess I ever saw in my life. They would send us money and then if we got a little settlement from something else, they'd sue us to get it back. Insurance Company of North America (INA) said, "You got your money now, so pay us what we paid you." And that was after we'd been paying them premiums for years! When we were trying to get money through our insurance protection plan, we had to go through their doctor all the time to get that. Answer questions, prove this, prove that. They were awful. After we moved to Oklahoma they always had somebody hanging around watching Charlie. The detectives even questioned neighbors about him. Pretty nasty people.

HENRY

So the INA threw a lien against me. When we went to the hearing, the judge tossed it out of court and said that INA wasn't entitled to that money. They still had people looking at me, watching me all time. Asking neighbors. I guess they thought I'd go out and start sprinting or playing ball. I could hardly walk much less anything else.

After it was thrown out, the one guy kept watching me all the time. He called up one time, trying to change his voice and I knew who he was and I questioned him about it, he said, "Henry, all I am is a go-between."

I told him, "You're asking all my neighbors about me." My neighbors always helped me out, you know. They chewed him out, even. Then I told him, "You know that cane I use all the time? Next time I see you, I'm gonna put it right between your ears." And I hung up.

Not long after we were in Goodner's grocery store and I said, "There's that bastard in the bread aisle." He looked at me and knew I saw him. After that I never saw him again.

CHAPTER FIVE

Reclaiming Roots

Henry and Fern found happiness after returning to Oklahoma. Once again, they were close to family, friends, and Comanche politics and powwows. Henry's interest in tribal affairs, however, waned and surged, depending on the political entities in power. His attitude is not uncommon, as Comanche politics are often volatile, and according to tribal members, the politicians are often self-serving.

Traditionally, the tribe consisted of approximately thirteen bands, with each band led by a headman who in turn was advised by a council. Bands cooperated with each other, but there was no overall tribal leader. Headmen were chosen because the people respected their wisdom and bravery, but that leader did not make unilateral decisions. Decisions were based on the needs of the bands or tribe, not on the needs of one faction or a few individuals.

After contact with Europeans, the unity of many tribes broke down due to the interference of missionaries and U.S. policies that dictated how tribes should function. Colonialism undermined traditional gender roles; for example, women in many tribes once had substantial social, political, economic, and religious power and respect. When patriarchal thought, which included the introduction of Christianity and the nuclear family (that God is male and men should be heads of the monogamous households), was adopted by tribespeople, tribal cultures changed dramatically.[1] Many Indians, however, did not desire to adopt the ways of white society and preferred to remain traditional, that is, to speak their language, practice their religious ceremonies, marry other Indians, and adhere to their tribal traditions. This disparity in cultural adherences among members of the same tribe caused rifts in all tribes, and those conflicts continue.

Today, the Comanche Indian Tribe, consisting of five thousand Comanches living near the Lawton area, is a federally recognized tribe that is governed by a chairperson (so far, only men) and a business committee. Elections are held to determine the chair and the council. As LaDonna Harris, Stephen M. Sachs, and Benjamin J. Broome have observed in their essay "Wisdom of the People: Potential and Pitfalls in Efforts by the Comanches to Recreate Traditional Ways of Building Consensus," "those who lose an election often feel that they have been rejected by the community, and feel that their honor has been impugned. People who are not included in the making of a decision, even if they are invited to a meeting to state their opinion to the decision makers, tend to feel left out."[2] The essay also observes that the tribe suffers from "infighting and lack of adequate participation by tribal members in the governance process."[3] After 1994, especially, "infighting returned to the tribe, perhaps more vehemently than before . . . Comanches felt themselves divided and often paralyzed in deciding major issues, partly because of the clash in values between their traditional culture and the premises of the contemporary governmental processes, which are based for the most part upon modern European-American understandings."[4]

Despite the frustrations Henry feels about his tribe's politics, he perseveres and continues to vote and attend meetings.

HENRY

I've been getting away from Comanche politics. I got disgusted with it. They can't get along, and them in the government fight among themselves and bump heads with each other. We have some real characters in the tribe. A few years ago a lady named McClung barricaded herself in the tribal complex. The new chairman had been voted in, but she said they voted her in. She stayed inside and wouldn't come out, and finally the tribal police got her out of there and arrested her.

I used to get commodities from the tribe and I don't even do that any more. I really don't need them, but it gripes me 'cause everyone else gets them. And a lot of people who live far away from the Comanche District get commodities. They say they live in the district, but they don't.

I go to meetings and listen to whoever's speaking, and sometimes I go vote but usually I mail it in. I go get my vehicle tags, and our cars have the Comanche plates on them instead of the Oklahoma ones. I like the Chairman, Johnny Wauqua. I talked to him a lot. He used to be an educational administrator, and he'd help the kids go to school. I know him real well. Seems most everybody supports him. I read the tribal newspaper whenever I get a copy. We also go to the homecomings. There's one this weekend. In October they have the Comanche Fair at Craterville.[5] I don't dance although I enjoy listening to them sing and watching them dance. We went when they dedicated the Comanche Veterans. And then they had a dedication for a guy I was raised up with, Thomas Chockpoyah. He was killed in Europe.

The tribal police is usually at the headquarters, but they also have the BIA police. When Del [Adele] worked there during one election in the 1980s, they had rifles, and she said that some people who were from the other political faction shot into the building. I took my rifle up there too and sat in her office until things calmed down. I just get too worked up over the tribe's politics and I don't have any interest in running. About the only reason I like going up there is because of that Comanche language class.[6]

One time one of my sisters got mad at me and said, "You're not my brother anymore," 'cause I supported the other candidate. But I thought I was in the right. I also knew this one lady, her name was Sarah Saddle Blanket, who got on me like a duck on a June bug about being on the opposite political side from her. I went over to talk to her husband, and Sarah—she's supposed to be distant kin—started getting all over me, saying I shouldn't be on her side of the building if I was gonna vote for the other guy. She was getting mad and so I left, but first I said, "We all need to be one group, not fighting among ourselves."

Then she said, "I don't want to hear it."

And I told her anyway, "That guy you're voting for doesn't have enough sense to pour piss out of a boot." And man, she came off that chair. Her husband started laughing and then she got onto him and I walked away. The tribe needs to do more for the poor ones, the older ones, and the kids. Comanches need to watch out for each other and take care of each other, and we don't do enough of that.

FERN

We'd go out there to Comanche meetings when we got back, but things got so hectic with the tribe, them arguing all the time, so we gave up on them for a while. For years all they did was fight with each other, and it was real disgusting. I think it's finally getting straightened out. I told Charlie for years to run for office over there, but he always said, "Oh, I couldn't do that." He's too concerned about everyone's welfare to be a politician.

Although Henry continues to rely on a leg brace to stabilize his knee, he still actively hunts, fishes and walks across his "home place" at least three times a week. He likes to drive and four to five times a year he and Fern make the fourteen-hour trek to visit us in Flagstaff. Until his long-time best friend, Ron

Halpin, died three years ago, Henry traveled to Colorado every fall to hunt elk and deer. Along with playing with his grandchildren and visiting with his relatives and friends, Henry's deepest joy is to sit and watch animals on his land. Sadly, Henry's allotment is land-locked. A wealthy white landowner who has bought all the Indian allotment parcels around Henry forces him to drive across others' property in order to get to his.

Henry is not the only Indian in Oklahoma to own land that is surrounded by non-Indians. Foster reports that by 1950, Comanches, Kiowas and Kiowa-Apaches lost more than fifty percent of the land that had been allotted to them, and thirty years later, forty percent of those remaining lands were gone. The population of the three tribes, however, had tripled.[7]

FERN

I was feeling better mentally once we got back to Oklahoma. Charlie felt better in Oklahoma, too, because we were close to relatives. In 1973, we bought a house in Duncan, and my mama and dad were still living then and his relatives were still around close, and the farm was out there and he could just go out to it. Not like in California where you'd have to drive miles and miles and miles to even get to the country. He could just go out there to the home place. And so many of his friends lived back here, and when we first moved back we were real happy to be back there among people we knew. I definitely was. I always wanted to get back close to my mom and dad. I went out to the country with Charlie when we first moved back, but I didn't go out there as much as him.

HENRY

That allotted land belonged to my mother. When she died in 1932, it went to me and my dad. One allotment, 160 acres. When I go out there today, I just feel good about it. I come out here two or three times a week. Sometimes Fern comes with me and she reads a book in the truck while I sit and watch animals, like armadillos, coons, turkeys, deer, or I fish. I'll come back from walking around and Fern will say, "You missed the deer that just walked by."

That land means everything to me. It's my connection to the tribe, to my family, and to the earth. My family will always have the home place because we won't sell it no matter how much the white people want to pay for it. I have so many memories of my family and friends and the time we spent together under the arbor in the hot summers and in the old house in the winters.

I like to study stuff out here, like what all these tracks are. And I want to see animals out here. I enjoy hunting them, too, but you can't kill them all at once. One old guy in town was telling me I could kill all the quail on my place in one year and they'd come back the next year. I told him, "Bull—they aren't gonna come back. You gotta put a bunch of other birds out there to take their place."

I spend so much time here hunting and fishing, and I brought Kim out here whenever we could. Like you do with Tosh out in the woods in Flagstaff. Look around for tracks, birds, try to identify trees. When I was little I used to ride an old plow horse named Syd around here and do the same thing. Syd was supposed to just work at plowing, and then I rode him and Dad didn't like that.

Not too long ago pecans were forty-five cents a pound, so me and my friend Jim came out here and we thought, "Boy, we're gonna make us some money," and we came out here and filled three tote sacks full of pecans, and when we took them into town they were twenty-seven cents a pound. So gall dang, we just started giving those things out to everyone.

I keep a feeder out there to feed the deer and turkeys. Sometimes I put out apples and man, they're gone in an hour. Most of those animals on my property, like deer, turkeys, bobcats, belong to the state and roam different properties. If a hunter has permission to hunt on my property, then they can, but if not, I call the tribal police. But nine times out of ten they're gone when the tribal police get there. I got signs up and run them out when I can. The police say to write their tag number down and then turn it over to tribal police and then they know who's out there and talk to them.

And it's up to the landowner. I'm trying to keep people out of there but I'm having problems, they just keep coming there. I got a creek and since I keep people out fairly well, I got more animals on my land than most have.

I come out here with a Coke and sit down and just enjoy it. I was gonna build me another house out here with chickens and an old horse to ride around on, but one of my sisters messed me up. Long time ago I had bought five acres from her and she backed out of the deal after I paid her. Her husband was active in the tribal council. They got all that land from Dad when they were taking care of him. My brother-in-law was the instigator on that; he was pretty sharp. What they did was talk to Dad when he was sick, then they took him up to the BIA and Dad deeded to land over to my sister, and by rights it should have been my brother Roy's land. They said they deserved it because they were taking care of Dad, you see. She already got her property—160 acres. But they got that and Roy didn't get nothing. She got her share and half her mother's share and her daddy's share.

When we lived in California, I told her I wanted to buy five acres off her place on the north side and she said okay. We were going to have the Comanche tribe build us a house, but it had to be on the roadway part of the allotment. My land was on the backside. So I paid her for five acres and I trusted her that she'd go and change the deed. All she had to do was go over to Anadarko and just deed that over to me. And I always thought that she did. And then we come back, and I asked her about it and she said, "Well, [my husband] said it was taking too much of our land and I never done it."

I said, "I want my money now. With interest."

She said, "I don't have it."

And I told her "You better get it." And she did, but not with interest. They went and borrowed it somewhere, I don't know where. The way me and Fern figured it out, her husband's the one who told her it was too much land—five acres.

Stella got her own land. In 1907 or thereabouts when the Indians got their sections, I guess some of my brothers and sisters were still alive and they got land. When they were small and passed away, it went back to my folks. And they even got land over on the Big Pasture, west of Lawton. And then they got land in Devol and Grandfield.[8] See, my brother Johnny had 160 acres, and when he died, that land went to Jody. She was half Indian, just like Kim. She was Comanche and half white. She's the one who died about ten years ago in Tucson. And then when she died, it went to Melody. They still got that property out there, but I don't know how long they'll have it. That's the reason I wanted to keep this little land I got and give it to these grandkids here. Kim'll be the executor until they're of age. Fern will have land use right until she dies, then it goes to the grandkids.

I willed it to Adele and Kim. Me and Fern talked about it and I wanted to keep it on the Mihesuah side. If it went to a white side of the family, then they got to pay taxes on it. Unless you're a member of another tribe like you [Choctaw] and you wouldn't have to pay taxes.

The tribe doesn't regulate what we do on our land. We can do whatever we want to. No building permits or anything. Like if you lease it to somebody and they write down that they're gonna put something on it and that they'll take it off when the lease is over, then they have to. But if they build a fence or put up a building, then they can't move it if it's not in the contract. It stays there as part of the property.

The same guy who bought up all the land around me is waiting to buy our land so he can drill. He'd buy it in a second. If we had a well, there's no telling what you might hit, but then we'd have to pay for the well. I'd like you all to buy Indian land. You'll have an income the rest of your life and you won't have to pay taxes or nothing on it. If gold or something else valuable was discovered on that land, the tribe couldn't have a part of it.

I can go back to the place where I was born, and most people can't do that. I go to the cemetery and I just go out there and sit. I just feel good. It seems like I'm with my folks out there. Lots of people know about the place 'cause lots of families got graves out there. Fern and I and them Eschiti boys always cleaned it up. James Jr. ["Jimmy"] just died this spring, but his brothers Lewis, Edward, and Leonard and I'll keep it up. We go out there and mow it, and my niece, who thinks she's always right, claims that it's never cleaned up, which is not true. It's cleaned up all the time.

When I was growing up colored people needed a place to be buried. A little baby died and the city of Temple wouldn't let them bury it there. So Jimmy Eschiti told them they could bury their baby out there at the home place. Now there's a little colored boy buried out there by the big old tree, and it isn't marked. There's some Mexicans, too, on the outside of the cemetery.

If you're buried out there, the same rules apply like if you were in the city, except you don't need a vault. The family has to dig the grave. And the tribe doesn't assist with the cost of burial. Nobody really knows where everybody is buried. Some are marked and some aren't. Joe Johnson brought a big white rock out there for Eschiti's grave. But they never put it on there or marked on it. It's outside the gates now. Most have tombstones or flat markers. There's room for more people to be buried out there, but some of those tombstones aren't marked, and there may be someone buried and not marked at all. It looks like there's a space between Martha and my mother. Those were Roy's two babies buried there, but there's no markers.

I used to want to be in Eschiti's cemetery, but not now. Fern's dad bought me a gravesite in Duncan cemetery near him and Fern's mother because he wanted me to be buried beside them. That don't matter, go ahead. I don't care where I'm buried, really. I don't know if I can get in there next to Fern. It looks like a space for a little baby plot where they're gonna put me. My brother Roy, he wanted to be buried out there in the family cemetery right by the gate so he can see who comes in and out. Stella and them didn't want him there so they took him to the Deyo Mission and buried him over there. In a roundabout way they claimed he didn't clean it up, so he couldn't be buried there. They gripe all the time about it and never do a thing.

FERN

Lorine Gibson Porter wanted her and her third husband's ashes scattered on Charlie's land. She's the one who lived in Duncan and out by the home place when she was little girl. On an allotment—Jimmy and them's—and she called Charlie and asked if she could have her ashes scattered out there when she died. And she still had her third husband's ashes. Charlie told her yes. We used to go see her all the time, and she called Charlie to talk quite a bit. She knew everything about Charlie's family. Even the ones who had died. And she wrote all this down.

She got real sick and went to live with her daughters in the last years of her life in the state of Washington, and they finally called us and told us she had passed away. The next year they'd bring her and her husband's ashes down and have a little ceremony to scatter the ashes.

So they called and told us when they were coming. Her daughter and her husband were the ones having the ceremony. And her son and his wife came too. They all came over to the house and they brought Charlie a peace pipe that we smoked out there. Some Indian made it. A home-made deal, you know. An Indian from Washington State told them what to do for the ceremony.

They tried to light the sweet grass and the rain kept putting it out. It was wet and it was cold! It was wintertime, sleeting and everything. They even took their shoes off in the rain. Well, this Indian guy had told them not to dishonor the dead in the cemetery and so they took off their shoes.

HENRY

Sometimes I go on others' property. I got keys to their gates, but I have to go through there in order to get to my property. You know there's a problem with my land. There's no easement to my property and I have to drive across someone else's land to get to mine. I talked to this other lawyer about it and he said we really need to get an easement through there. Later on it'll be hard to do, or to even get access to the property. The white land owner's got it blocked off.

That white man—a *taivo*—bought all that Indian land around me. A lot of it belonged to people in my family. They sold it off and then they had nothing. If I had known my family was gonna sell off their land, I would have bought it. But they never gave family opportunity to buy it, and that tears me up. It really makes me mad at how stupid they are. Like my sister, I told her not to get all her lease money at once. I told her, "Let him pay you monthly; if you get it all at once, it's gonna be gone." They could raise the lease, too, but they never thought of that.

That *taivo*'s got it pretty well blocked off now. My sisters Hilda and Stella, they have property straight across the creek from mine. And it borders next to mine and his land. Eschiti was on the north end. The Eschitis had more than a square mile. I don't know if it was someone in that *taivo*'s family, but someone burned down that bridge that goes across Little Beaver Creek, which was the road I always used. They never did replace it. When we left for California we had it leased out to them and they didn't maintain the road like they used to, but it was still there all the time. That *taivo* bought enough sections so he blocked me off and we couldn't get through there. I talked to the county commissioner about who authorized the closing the road, and now he's saying there was never a road there and that's not true. I used to be on it all the time.

Adele helps me a lot, and I talked to her about it and she said, "Daddy, what you need to do is write letters to everybody. The governor, the President, the BIA, everybody." So we wrote and everybody answered me, but nobody wanted to help me. The only one who really wanted to help me was Governor Boren of Oklahoma. The assistant attorney had written Boren and said he'd like to talk to me and explain everything to me about that place out there. Because, according to him, there was never a road out there. And then Boren sent me a copy of the letter this attorney wrote him. So I read it and made an appointment to go down and talk to him.

So I went to the Soil and Moisture down in Walters 'cause they all know me and I told them what the problem was. They said he can't block me from my land. They said somebody told him to close that road off and he can't do that. Anyway, I said I want to get a map and they gave me one. When I went down there to meet with the district attorney I took Fern's cousin with me as a witness. And I underlined everything I wanted him to explain to me. And he couldn't explain nothing. I showed him on the map where that road runs. And I showed him right where the house is and how the road runs right up to it and a little past it. I said, "There's a road there since I was a child. I'm seventy-nine years old. There's a mail route there. The mail comes through there."

But he didn't know what to say 'cause he didn't know the facts. Same with the BIA and their attorneys from Tulsa who called me. They told the district attorney there was no existing road and I had to get permission from the land owner to go to my property. You see, they don't know.

It's all politics. It has nothing to do with what I know or what happened. It's all politics. That *taivo* is rich and he pays them all off. He's a powerful man in Stephens County. One of the richest ones there with his oil and everything. And what ever you tell a politician, if you give them money, he's gonna do it. They do know. And like Josh says, "They're screwing you."

The people in Duncan who are telling me the wrong things may know someone in the BIA. That's how that guy gets all that land. He pays for people to run for senate, governor. He can pull strings everywhere. He's so powerful he won't let anyone help me.

Everybody knows there was a road there. And if I really wanted to get serious, then I can get a lawyer and find it in the records somewhere. Old maps. It'll cost a fortune and he has the money to burn me out and he knows it. He can pay them off. Well, Josh is gonna have to deal with him soon. And the tribe won't help.

★ ★ ★

I keep saying "Indian" but "Comanche" is what I mean. Tribes aren't the same. Me and Fern stop in Winslow whenever we come see you in Flagstaff, and whenever we walk into a restaurant all them "Nava-joes" just stare. I speak but they won't answer. They just look over your head like you don't exist 'cause you're not one of them.

I wish I knew more of the Comanche language. Like I told my buddy Ray Niedo who was on the trip with me to Adobe Walls last year, "If I was around you a while, I'd learn to talk Comanche." I can understand most of it but can't say it back as well. I enjoy being with the people who're trying to teach the language.

I've always known I was Comanche, but to white people, Comanches and other Indians are all the same. A lot of people are just wannabee Comanches. You are what you are. You can always put on and pretend you're Indian, you know. A lot of people do that all the time. I know who I am. I'm Comanche and I don't need Indian stuff in my house to prove it. We never did have Comanche things in our house growing up and we were all Indians. People like to collect stuff, but we don't.

One time, when I was going to see Ron Halpin in Colorado where we hunted all the time, I stopped in New Mexico at a place that advertised cheap gas. So I thought, "Well, I'll fill up all my saddle tanks." They didn't have any signs up saying which island was which, so I just took off the gas cap and the guy comes walking out of the store and says, "Hey, you Goddamn Navajo. What do you think you're doing?" Just like that.

And I said, "What do you mean? I'm putting gas in here."

"That's a priority pump, Indian," he says. "We do the pumping there. You go on over on that side there."

I put the cap back on the pickup and put the hose up and walked over to him. "I don't know how to talk to people around here, but I'm equal to you and you aren't gonna call me a Goddamn Navajo again and if you do, then me and you are gonna be waltzing all over the place. I'm Comanche."

Well, then he apologizes. I just got in my truck and drove off. A person like that, why would he say something like that? Maybe because there were so many Navajos around there he can talk to them that way and they do nothing about it. I guess I could have taken him to court for discrimination.

★   ★   ★

There's people not Comanche by blood, but who know the language and culture, like Cynthia Ann Parker. She may have claimed she was Comanche after living with them so long, but I think she was still white. Her son Quanah was half-Comanche and half-white, but he's Comanche. If a person is half-blood, it depends on the culture they follow, and Quanah followed the Comanche side for most of his life.

Appearance makes a difference too. There was this kid who went with us to Adobe Walls, and I'd say he was about maybe twelve years old. And he was colored. Or half colored. He said he was part Indian. I listened to these other guys who come from Santa Fe talk about him. And they said he was *twotywa*—that's "black" in Comanche. So see, they first saw him and he looks colored. His hair's kinky and he tried to make a ponytail out of it, you know, and he still looks colored and that's how people see him. Most people still go by his appearance.

Being a Comanche to me means being connected to my past, being close to my family and to the land and animals, the earth, and the plants we grew and harvested. I hunt but I respect the animals I kill. When I was younger and had to hunt for food, I rode my horse Skeeter, and while I hunted for squirrels and rabbits with my bow I pretended I was a Comanche warrior. All those skills I learned from my father, who learned them from Mihesuah. I was born to hunt and fish, and I could live off the land if I had to. Like my ancestors, the men and women. I really enjoyed growing up out there. I didn't have nothing and either walked or rode a horse. We had a brush arbor and we did everything under that thing in the summer when it was hot: cook, sleep, eat. It wasn't much, but it was my home place and still is.

I pray that my grandchildren will have a connection to their history and culture, and I hope they have the same feelings about the land. Living in the forest where you do helps gives them that respect. That's why I left my allotment to Toshaway and Ariana so someday they can share it with their children and grandchildren.

People don't have connections with the land anymore. They stay away from their family and keep to themselves. Being Comanche means being part of the tribe and working with the land and animals. If everyone lived a simpler life, we'd be in better shape.

Fern tells me I need to get a little notebook and go around and talk to people so I can find out more about my family and history. There's this one old Indian lady I need to go see who told me once that I'm part Shoshone. She's only about four feet tall. I need to find out what she meant by that. She was always over by the grocery store over in Lawton. I'd get a lot more truth out of her than I can from some members of my family who think they know everything but don't. I don't know why I didn't ask more questions when I was younger. Those old ones could have told me a lot of things. I just wasn't interested back then. Now I am, but it's too late to ask questions.

Notes

INTRODUCTION

1. For general works on the Comanches, see Bannon, *Spanish Borderlands*; Fehrenbach, *The Comanches*; Hagan, *United States–Comanche Relations*; Wallace and Hoebel, *The Comanches*; John, *Storms Brewed*; Kavanagh, *The Comanches*; Noyes, *Los Comanches*; and Pritzker, *Native American Encyclopedia*. For information on the Texas Historical Commission's Red River War Archaeological Project, contact the Archaeology Division, Texas Historical Commission, P.O. Box 12276, Austin, Texas, 78711–2276. For information on Comanche society, culture, and politics, see Foster, *Being and Becoming Comanche*.

2. Leonard "Black Moon" Riddles is married to Henry's niece, Eva May, who is the daughter of Henry's oldest sibling, May Portillo. Riddles is an alumnus of Fort Sill Indian School and has been painting since he was a child. He is now considered one of the most outstanding Native artists, and his works hang in galleries from New York to Phoenix.

3. I included the essay by Elizabeth Cook-Lynn in the collection *Natives and Academics* because I understand and appreciate her comments.

4. See Deloria Jr., "Comfortable Fictions and the Struggle for Turf."

5. Hamilton, *Sentinel of the Southern Plains*, 126, 127, 132.

6. See Bataille and Silet, *Pretend Indians*; Hanson and Rouse, "Dimensions of Native American Stereotyping"; Hanson and Rouse, "American Indian Stereotyping"; Hirschfelder, *American Indian Stereotypes*; Marsden and Nachbar, "The Indian in the Movies"; Mihesuah, *American Indians*; and Stedman, *Shadows of the Indians*.

7. Catlin, *Letters and Notes*, 496–97.

8. Webb, *The Great Plains*, 65.

9. "Joshua Glad His Girls Are to be Given Education at U.S. Expense," *Duncan Weekly Eagle*, May, 16, 1935.

10. See for example, Eggan, *The American Indian*; Foster, *Being and Becoming Comanche*; and Linton, *Acculturation in Seven American Indian Tribes*.

11. See Stonequist, *Marginal Man*.

12. See McFee, "The 150% Man."

13. Isaacs, *Idols of the Tribe*, 79.

14. Yellowbird, "What We Want To Be Called." It is preferable to refer to the indigenous people of this country by their specific tribal names, and I personally prefer "indigenous." But in this book, I opt for "American Indians" or "Indians" (instead of "Native Americans," which signifies anyone born in the United States). I am well aware of the debates over these terms and am cognizant that many find "Indian" offensive; however, my family, including Henry, and most "Indians" I know say "Indian." Terms such as "First Nations" and others are fine for scholars, but most Indians, especially older ones, are puzzled at hearing them.

1. FAMILY

1. Pritzker, *Native American Encyclopedia*, 309–10.

2. Both accounts are in Jones, *Sanapia*, 6–7.

3. Comanches and Kiowas may have had an historic alliance, but today, when talking to Comanches about Kiowas, a common attitude is that "Kiowas copied our culture." It is interesting to note how difficult it is to distinguish Kiowas from Comanches in historic photographs; the Smithsonian Institution Anthropological Archives, for example, has hundreds of unidentified photographs, many labeled "Comanche?" and "Kiowa?"

4. The best work on Cynthia Ann Parker is Hacker, *Cynthia Ann Parker*. Parker (1827–1870) was the daughter of Silas and Lucy Parker. In 1832 the family moved from Illinois to Texas with part of the congregation of the Primitive Baptist Church, which was led by Cynthia's uncle, Elder John Parker. Their settlement, known as Fort Parker, was fortified against Indian attacks by walls. In 1836, Caddo, Comanche, and Kiowa warriors attacked Fort Parker and captured five settlers. All were eventually returned to their families except for Cynthia Ann, who had quickly assimilated to Comanche life. She married Peta Nocona, a Quahada Comanche leader. They had three children: Quanah, Pecos, and Topsannah. In 1860, she was captured by whites after Lawrence Sullivan Ross attacked Nacona's camp on the Pease River. She and Topsannah were taken to Camp Cooper, where she was identified by her uncle; she subsequently went to live with him on his farm in Birdville, Texas. Shortly afterward, she learned that Pecos died from smallpox; Topsannah then died from influenza. Cynthia Ann remained unhappy the rest of her life and died in 1870 from depression and self-inflicted starvation.

The legacy of Cynthia Ann Parker lives on in Texas, especially around Parker County. Conversations with residents reveal that a good portion of the white population claim they are descendants of Cynthia Ann. Since Quanah was her only offspring to reproduce, any claimant would be part Comanche. Ironically, many of the people I spoke with throughout the years I lived in Fort Worth do not care to be part Comanche, so they say, "No, I'm from her white side." Like the thousands of "wannabes" who assert that they have a Cherokee princess for a grandmother, being a descendant of Cynthia Ann Parker gives whites an opportunity to connect with Native America. Some Cherokees, for example, are known for being "civilized" and looking phenotypically white and are therefore a "safe" tribe to claim. Cynthia Ann was culturally Comanche, but not racially Indian. She is, therefore, a safe connection to the savage past.

On the racial and cultural identities of Cherokees and why so many non-Indians claim to be Cherokee, see Mihesuah, *Cultivating the Rosebuds*. On how Indians and non-Indians formulate Indian identities, see Mihesuah, "American Indian Identities."

5. The Battle of Adobe Walls historical marker is located north of Stinnett, Texas, in the state's panhandle on State Highway 207 at the junction with State Highway 136. The six-acre tract of land in Hutchinson County where the site is located is owned by the Panhandle-Plains Historical Society. Henry was one of over a dozen Comanches who traveled to the Adobe Walls battlefield as part of a tour sponsored by the Comanche Language and Cultural Preservation Committee and the Panhandle Plains Museum. One Comanche visitor remarked that "This is a family pilgrimage to a very hallowed piece of ground as far as we're concerned." Jeanne Grimes, "Family to Make Trip Into Past," *Lawton Constitution*, June 23, 1999.

6. In Noyes, *Los Comanches*, 308, the injured man's name is "Howea." However, Noyes gives no source for this information other than that his shooting was witnessed by "besieged buffalo hunters."

7. Tenskwatawa, the Shawnee prophet, for example, told his people in the early nineteenth century that if they performed dances and ceremonies in a certain fashion, and stopped drinking, using material goods brought by whites, and burning tribespeople accused of witchcraft, God would send the whites away and life would return to its traditional state. The Pauite prophet Wovoca, a man who claimed to have died during an eclipse of the sun and spoken with God, brought the Ghost Dance to the plains in the 1880s. Wovoca claimed that if Indians performed the Ghost Dance, whites would disappear, the buffalo would return, and dead tribespeople would be brought to life. The Ghost Shirts the dancers wore would supposedly deflect the white men's bullets. Minneconjous who performed the Ghost Dance at Pine Ridge in 1890 were the victims of the massacre at Wounded Knee. Others with similar messages are Kenekuk, the Kickapoo prophet, and Handsome Lake, the Seneca prophet. See "American Indian Prophets"; Edmunds, *Shawnee Prophet*; Herring, *Kenekuk*; Miller, *Prophetic Worlds*; and Mooney, *The Ghost-Dance Religion*.

8. Among the sources that incorrectly refer to White Eagle as Eschiti prior to the Battle of Adobe Walls are Brown and Schmitt, *Fighting Indians*, 64; Fehrenbach, *The Comanches*, 533; Hagan, *United States–Comanche Relations*, 105; Kenner, *History of New Mexican–Plains Indian Relations*, 204; Wallace and Hoebel, *The Comanches*, 319; Kavanagh, *The Comanches*, 51, 445–46; Kavanaugh, *Comanche Political History*, 450; Nye, *Carbine and Lance*, 191; Noyes and Gelo, *Comanches in the New West*, 5; Stockel, *LaDonna Harris*, 5; and Thrapp, *Encyclopedia of Frontier Biography*, 708. Nye, Noyes and Gelo, and Thrapp assert that in regards to "Isa-tai's" prediction of the outcome at Adobe Walls, the Comanches forgave him and forgot the incident. They did not; hence his name change from White Eagle to Eschiti.

These errors reveal one of the problems of researching topics in indigenous studies: many indigenous scholars do not use informants to acquire information. They cite each other, use the same references, and do not incorporate indigenous voices. Even when one does use indigenous voices, one must be careful to make certain that the voice is authoritative, that is, that they know what they're talking about. Two books on Comanches use Comanche voices: Stockel's *LaDonna Harris* (although she cites the incorrect reference) and Foster's *Being and Becoming Comanche*. On the debates over how scholars write about Indians, see Mihesuah, *Natives and Academics*.

9. For information (purely from the non-Indian perspective) on Mackenzie, see Carter, *On the Border With Mackenzie*; Wallace, "Ranald Slidell Mackenzie"; and Wallace, "Prompt in the Saddle."

10. Most people believe that Quanah brought the peyote religion to the Southwest. There are, however, many versions of how peyote arrived. According to several sources, in the late 1870s or early 1880s, Quanah traveled to Chihuahua to visit his non-Indian relatives. He became very ill after a bull gored him and infection took hold. His grandmother sent for a *curandera*, a Mexican female healer. Among the treatments she supplied was a bitter tea made from peyote, a portion of a cactus that Indians of Mexico had used for centuries in rituals. Quanah believed that the peyote tea cured him. He accompanied the *curandera* to Mexican Indian religious ceremonies in which participants drank peyote tea or ate the cactus buttons (which initially make one dizzy and nauseated, then subsequently euphoric and content) in order to "connect" to God. Another version is that news of peyote was brought to the Comanche tribe by Apaches, who had been exposed to the religion for some time. See Foster, *Being and Becoming Comanche*, 92–96, 189 n. 76.

Regardless of its origin, peyote was quickly embraced by numerous tribes. Arapahos, Caddos, Cheyennes, Delawares, and Pawnees adopted the ceremony, known as the "Comanche Way," "Quanah Parker Rite," and "Half Moon Ceremony." In 1918, the Native American Church was founded in Oklahoma with the purpose of promoting "the Christian religion with the practice of the Peyote Sacrament." Peyotists argue that they are able to speak to entities such as Jesus, the Great Spirit, and Mother Earth.

Today, peyote is in short supply. It is used not only by the approximately two hundred thousand members of the Native American Church but also by non-Indians wishing to get "high." The abuse of peyote is such a problem that in Texas, individuals who wish to use peyote legally in Native American Church ceremonies must prove that they are at least one-quarter Indian blood, which also means they must be tribally enrolled. In addition, the Bureau of Indian Affairs and the U.S. Department of Education recognize as Indians only those who are recognized by such a tribe. See "A Saint of South Texas: Retired Peyote Dealer Remains a Symbol of Hope for a Misunderstood Faith," *Dallas Morning News*, March 15, 1997; "Congress Considers Native American Church Pleas on Peyote Use," *Dallas Morning News*, June 20, 1994.

Although the Native American Church has spread throughout the Southwest and many Navajos actively participate in the ritual, my Navajo students say that some traditional Navajos will not participate in the Native American Church because they see it as a Comanche ceremony, and they will not take part in "their enemies' " rituals.

For further information on peyote, see Martin, *Native American Religion*, 108–19; and Stewart, *Peyote Religion*.

11. As Morris Foster points out in *Being and Becoming Comanche*, there exists the "myth of Quanah" (187). Parker was not, as William Hagan (1980) has written, the "war leader" in the pre-reservation period. His reputation as chief of all Comanches is due partly to the "Cynthia Ann mystique" as well as to the admonitions of Indian agents and other whites who used him as a middleman. He never served as the tribe's chief; rather, he was one of several successful intermediary leaders. Descendants of Quanah maintain the myth of Quanah as chief, while those not related often refer to him as a "sellout" because of his ability to reap economic profit from the Indian agencies that distributed annuities.

12. According to Lorine Gibson, when she was a child she witnessed a few exchanges about Mumsuki:

> Joshua's brother-in-law Mum-seh-ki asked Papa to bring out a tombstone he had ordered to be placed at the grave of his wife's first husband . . . Mum-seh-ki, however, seemed to be something of a laughing stock among them [Comanches]. He made a great pretense of being a chief and medicine man by virtue of having married Isatai's widow. No one, either Indian or white, ever called Tahverti by any name other than Isatai.
>
> Papa brought the tombstone out from town. The inscription on it read: "When Chief Mum-seh-ki die he go see Isatai." The next time Papa saw Joshua he asked him if he had seen that stone. Joshua said he had not and Papa told him about the inscription. Joshua laughed and said, "You think he see him? Isatai good man. Mum-seh-ki kill his own brother, get his wife. No, I don't think he see him" ("A Plains Family," 80–81).

Henry comments that his father spoke grammatically correct English, not just disjointed phrases as recounted here and in the *Duncan Weekly Eagle*.

13. Fort Sill Indian School opened in 1871. See Centennial Booklet Committee, *Fort Sill Indian School*. At least one notable scholarly work, however, asserts that it did not open until twenty years later. See for example, Hagan, *United States–Comanche Relations*, 199–200. Henry has always been told by family members that his father was taken as a small child to attend Fort Sill Indian School. His father was born in 1874; if the school opened in the 1890s, he would have been in his twenties. Numerous other family members also attended the school.

14. See Wahhahdooah, *Deyo Mission*. The Baptist Deyo Mission was established in the fall of 1893, eight miles west of present-day Lawton. The first missionaries were the Rev. and Mrs. E. C. Deyo of New York. Henry's parents were baptized in 1905, and Henry and most of his siblings were baptized in the 1930s.

15. For information on boarding schools, see Adams, *Education for Extinction*;

Coleman, *American Indian Children*; Ellis, *To Change Them Forever*; Lomawaima, *They Called It Prairie Light*; McBeth, *Ethnic Identity*; Mihesuah, *Cultivating the Rosebuds*; Trennert, *The Phoenix Indian School*; and the video *In the White Man's Image*.

16. Between 1903 and 1911, Deyo Baptist Mission reported 150 Comanche converts. In 1920, there were thirteen churches among the Kiowa, Comanches, and Apaches, and 1,495 out of a population of 4,631 were members (Foster, *Being and Becoming Comanche*, 120–21).

17. Ibid., 121–22.

18. Cited in Foster, *Being and Becoming Comanche*, 101.

19. Comanche cultural change for this period is discussed in Foster, *Being and Becoming Comanche*, 100–130.

20. This is also an assertion of other students: "According to reports of older Indians, students were whipped for disobeying rules. Rev. Thomas Komah, of Bethany, Oklahoma, said the boys were whipped if they used their Indian language at school. Only English was permitted." Centennial Booklet Committee, *Fort Sill Indian School*, n.p.

21. Lorine Gibson's impression of Carrie Mihesuah is documented in "A Plains Family": "We were welcomed into the kitchen where Joshua's wife Carrie was baking pumpkin pies and frying doughnuts. Carrie was very, very fat. She had kind eyes, a sweet smile, and a soft, soothing voice. I loved her on sight and loved her even more when she started feeding me the most delicious pies and doughnuts I've ever tasted and talked to me as if I were a real person and not just a kid" (76).

She also describes the first time she met Peahbo (which she incorrectly spells "Pehabo"):

> Pehabo was sitting under the arbor in the [Mihesuahs'] yard and did not come into the house while we were there. Joshua had told Papa that Pehabo could understand English and even speak it if it became necessary. But she refused to speak it and avoided situations where it might be required (78).
>
> She had spread a tarp on the ground and sat on it with her feet straight before her, and she held a haunch of beef between her knees. With a very sharp knife she was slicing almost paper-thin strips from the beef and laying them in a pan beside her. A clothesline outside of the arbor was almost filled with strips of beef she had hung in the sun to dry (79–80).

22. Although Henry is not certain who is in the cradleboard, it is probably his sister Martha. Lorine Gibson tells of observing Martha in the cradleboard when Martha was four months old and May was fourteen, Roy was six, Johnny was four, and Hilda was two:

> Martha was laced into her papoose cradle, which stood in a semi-upright position against the wall. . . . I thought Martha must be uncomfortable laced so tightly into that boot and standing almost upright against the wall, but

her little round brown face never puckered. Her bright eyes looked happy and interested as she watched the other children playing around her on the floor. Carrie admonished the children with an occasional soft "nah, nah." I always felt envious of the Indian children because their parents were so patient ("A Plains Family," 79).

23. Gibson also comments that in regards to the Mihesuahs' religious adherence

Joshua was often heard to make the statement, "I am a Jesus man myself." Joshua sometimes invited white preachers to hold revival meetings under his arbor. The first ice cream I ever tasted was made in huge freezers under that arbor at the close of one of those revivals ("A Plains Family," 81).

24. Faxon is a small town located approximately twelve miles southwest of Lawton and thirty miles southwest of Duncan on Highway 36 in Comanche County, close to Big Pasture. (Big Pasture is not acknowledged on most maps of Oklahoma.)

25. Lorine Gibson observed similar fashions in the early 1900s:

Most of the Indian men of Joshua's age (late thirties) wore long hair in braids intertwined with bright-colored yarn or ribbon. Many wore blankets, and all wore black ten-gallon hats. Their wives were known as "blanket squaws." Pehabo [Peahbo], Tahverti [Tuvette], and Carrie wore only Indian-style clothing. Their dresses consisted of a length of cotton material with a hole in the middle to slip over the head. Another length of fabric was wrapped around the waist sarong fashion. Their outer coverings were brightly-colored and patterned blankets worn like a shawl. If they were dressed up, they wore those blankets even in summer ("A Plains Family," 81).

26. Henry was not aware of his sisters' ceremonies because he was a toddler at the time, but Gibson recounts that the Mihesuah girls did undergo puberty ceremonies and that the girls wore ceremonial dresses ("A Plains Family," 81).

27. The Wichita Mountains Wildlife Refuge is located about seventeen miles northwest of Lawton and west of Medicine Park. The sixty-thousand-acre refuge includes the five-thousand-acre Charons Garden Wilderness Area, trails such as the Dog Run Hollow Trail, and Quanah Parker Lake. Bison and turkeys as well as other wildlife roam the refuge.

28. Noyes and Gelo, *Comanches in the New West*, 62, posits that the name "Treetop" in Comanche is "Paaduhhuhyahquetop." The photograph facing page 62 in that book features Henry's childhood friend Bert.

2. EARLY LIFE

1. "Vanishing red men" was a phrase used in the latter part of the nineteenth and early twentieth centuries in regards to the low population figures of American

Indians. It is estimated that at the turn of the century the population of Indians was at its nadir, about 250,000. Many non-Indians hoped that Indians would either disappear completely or would at least lose their cultural knowledge and learn to live in mainstream white society. That they wouldn't be accepted as equals, however, is another issue. See Thornton, *American Indian Holocaust*, 159.

2. For information on the Dawes Severalty Act, see *General Allotment Act*, U.S. *Statutes at Large* 24:366–91; and Getches, Wilkinson, and Williams Jr., *Federal Indian Law*, 190–206.

3. The tragedies associated with allotment are discussed in Debo, *And Still the Waters Run*.

4. Duncan is located in Stephens County, approximately eighty-one miles south of Oklahoma City. It was established in 1889; its original growth was based on agriculture, oil, and stock raising. Lawton, thirty miles west of Duncan, was established in 1901, six days after the opening by lottery of the Kiowa-Comanche Reservation. It is home to Fort Sill.

5. Stahl, "Farming Among the Kiowa," 222–23; Hagan, *United States–Comanche Relations*, 269. Foster reports in *Being and Becoming Comanche* (116) that Anglo settlers outnumbered Indians on the Kiowa-Comanche reservation by thirty-three to one.

6. Lorine Gibson's family leased the Peahbo property, owned by Henry's maternal grandmother Peahbo. Gibson describes the house as well-built and solid and writes that "Mama was mightily pleased with it." Her mother was especially happy with the brick foundation that prevented the wind from blowing up through the floor cracks ("A Plains Family," 75–79).

7. The "Dust Bowl" refers to the approximately one hundred million acres in Oklahoma and other plains states that suffered extensive wind erosion damage in the 1930s because of drought and overplanting.

8. Halliburton is the large company that designed the oil well cementing process for safeguarding wells. Based in Duncan, it operates numerous plants throughout the country.

9. Anadarko, sixty miles southwest of Oklahoma City and the seat of Caddo County, is named after the Anadarko Indians. As was Lawton, it was founded in 1901 after the Kiowa-Comanche and Wichita reservations were opened to white settlement. Numerous tribes hold regular powwows there.

3. SERVICE AS A MARINE

1. Holm, *Strong Hearts Wounded Souls*, 104.

2. During World War II, fourteen Comanches were chosen to train in Florida and then in England prior to the June 1944 landing at Normandy. Just as the Navajo Code Talkers did, the Comanches perfected an unbreakable code in their own language and were instrumental in helping the Allies win the war. As of October 1999, only one Comanche Code Talker was still living. In 1989, France honored the Comanche Code Talkers for their contribution with the Chevalier de L'Order National du Mérite.

Non-Navajos often express their frustration at not being recognized for their efforts during World War II as Code Talkers. See Mark Shaffer, "Non-Navajo Code Talkers Seeking Equal Recognition," *Arizona Republic*, January 6, 2001.

3. Holm, *Strong Hearts Wounded Souls*, 25.

4. RELOCATION

1. For information on termination and relocation, see Fixico, *Termination and Relocation*; Fixico, *Urban Indian Experience*; Getches, Wilkinson, and Williams Jr., *Federal Indian Law*, 229–50; Philip, *Termination Revisited*. See also "American Indians and the Urban Experience."

2. In 1924, the Bureau of Indian Affairs was established within the War Department, where there was less sympathy for Indians and more disparity in the ability to manage Indian affairs. In 1949 the BIA was moved to the Department of the Interior. Today it acts as an advisory agency for tribes desiring self-determination and is responsible for maintaining the trust relationship between tribes and the federal government.

3. Lurie, "Menominee Termination"; Peroff, *Menominee Drums*.

5. RECLAIMING ROOTS

1. There is a growing literature about the effects of colonialism on tribes, particularly the effects on gender roles. See, for example, the most recent: Allen, *The Sacred Hoop*; Anderson, *Chain Her by One Foot*; Devens, *Countering Colonization*; Jacobs, *Engendered Encounters*; Leacock, *Myths of Male Dominance*; Mihesuah, *Indigenous American Women*; Perdue, *Cherokee Women*; Powers, *Oglala Women*; Axtell, *The Invasion Within*, and Berkhofer, *Salvation and the Savage*, mainly discuss the effects of colonialism without mentioning women.

2. Harris, Sachs, and Broome, "Wisdom of the People."

3. Harris, "Wisdom," 1.

4. Harris, "Wisdom," 1.

5. Craterville, or Craterville Park, is an area filled with streams that includes a natural amphitheater. The All-Indian Fair took place at Craterville Park from 1924 to 1934, when it moved to Anadarko. Craterville adjoins the Wichita Mountains; Quanah Parker's "star home" is located one mile away.

6. Offered by NƗU MU TEKWAPUHA NOMNEETATU, The Comanche Language and Cultural Preservation Committee, P.O. Box 3610, Lawton OK 73502.

7. Foster, *Being and Becoming Comanche*, 134.

8. Devol is approximately thirty miles south of Lawton and five miles north of the Red River in Cotton County. Grandfield is six miles west of Devol on Highway 70 in Tillman County.

Bibliography

Adams, David Wallace. *Education for Extinction: American Indians and the Boarding School Experience, 1875–1928.* Lawrence: University Press of Kansas, 1995.

Allen, Paula Gunn. *The Sacred Hoop: Recovering the Feminine in American Indian Traditions.* Boston: Beacon Press, 1986.

"American Indian Prophets: Religious Leaders and Revitalization Movements." *American Indian Quarterly* 9 no. 3 (summer 1985).

"American Indians and the Urban Experience." *American Indian Culture and Research Journal* 22 no. 4 (1998).

Anderson, Karen. *Chain Her by One Foot: The Subjugation of Women in Seventeenth-Century New France.* New York: Routledge, 1991.

Axtell, James. *The Invasion Within: The Contest of Cultures in Colonial North America.* New York: Oxford University Press, 1985.

Bannon, John Francis. *The Spanish Borderlands Frontier, 1513–1821.* New York: Holt, Rinehart and Winston, 1970.

Bataille, Gretchen, and Charles P. Silet. *The Pretend Indians: Images of Native Americans in the Movies.* Ames: Iowa State University Press, 1980.

Berkhofer, Robert A. *Salvation and the Savage: An Analysis of Protestant Missions and American Indian Response, 1787–1862.* Lexington: University of Kentucky Press, 1965.

Brown, Dee, and Martin F. Schmitt, *Fighting Indians of the West.* New York: Ballantine Books, 1978.

Carter, Robert G. *On the Border With Mackenzie, or Winning West Texas from the Comanches.* 1935. Reprint, New York: Antiquarian Press, 1961.

Catlin, George. *Letters and Notes on the Manners, Customs, and Conditions of the North American Indians: Written During Eight Years' Travel (1832–1839) Amongst the Wildest Tribes of Indians in North America.* 2 vols. 1841. Reprint. New York: Dover, 1973.

Centennial Booklet Committee. *The Fort Sill Indian School Centennial, 1871–1971.* N.p, n.d.

Charlton, John B. *The Old Sergeant's Story: Winning the West from the Indians and Bad Men in 1870 to 1876, by Captain Robert G. Carter.* New York: F. H. Hitchcock, 1926.

Clifton, James, ed. *The Invented Indian: Cultural Fictions and Government Policies.* New Brunswick, NJ: Transaction Publishers, 1990.

Coleman, Michael C. *American Indian Children at School, 1850–1930*. Jackson: University Press of Mississippi, 1993.

Cook-Lynn, Elizabeth. "American Indian Intellectualism and the New Indian Story," in *Natives and Academics: Researching and Writing About American Indians*, ed. Devon A. Mihesuah, 111–38. Lincoln: University of Nebraska Press, 1998.

Debo, Angie. *And Still the Waters Run: The Betrayal of the Five Civilized Tribes*. Princeton: Princeton University Press, 1940. Reprint, Norman: University of Oklahoma Press, 1984.

Deloria Jr., Vine. "Comfortable Fictions and the Struggle for Turf: An Essay Review of *The Invented Indian: Cultural Fictions and the Government Policies*." *American Indian Quarterly* 16 no. 3 (summer 1992): 399.

Devens, Carol. *Countering Colonization: Native American Women and Great Lakes Missions, 1630–1900*. Berkeley: University of California Press, 1992.

Edmunds, R. David. *The Shawnee Prophet*. Lincoln: University of Nebraska Press, 1983.

Eggan, Fred. *The American Indian: Perspectives for the Study of Social Change*. Chicago: Aldine, 1966.

Ellis, Clyde. *To Change Them Forever: Indian Education at the Rainy Mountain Boarding School, 1893–1920*. Norman: University of Oklahoma Press, 1996.

Fehrenbach, T. R. *The Comanches: The Destruction of a People*. New York: Knopf, 1974.

Fixico, Donald. *Termination and Relocation: Federal Indian Policy, 1945–1960*. Albuquerque: University of New Mexico Press, 1986.

———. *The Urban Indian Experience in America*. Albuquerque: University of New Mexico Press, 2000.

Foster, Morris. *Being and Becoming Comanche: A Social History of an American Community*. Tucson: University of Arizona Press, 1991.

General Allotment Act. U.S. *Statutes at Large* 24:366–91 (1887).

Getches, David H., Charles F. Wilkinson, and Robert A. Williams Jr. *Federal Indian Law: Cases and Materials*. 3d ed. St. Paul, MN: West, 1993.

Gibson, Lorine. "A Plains Family." Unpublished manuscript in possession of Gibson family.

Hacker, Margaret Schmidt. *Cynthia Ann Parker: The Life and Legend*. Texas Western Press Southwestern Studies, no. 92, December 1990.

Hagan, William T. *United States–Comanche Relations: The Reservation Years*. New Haven: Yale University Press, 1976.

———. "Quanah Parker," in *American Indian Leaders: Studies in Diversity*, ed. R. David Edumnds, 175–91. Lincoln: University of Nebraska Press, 1980.

Hamilton, Allen Lee. *Sentinel of the Southern Plains: Fort Richardson and the Northwest Texas Frontier, 1866–1878*. Fort Worth, TX: Texas Christian University Press, 1988.

Hanson, Jeffrey R., and Linda P. Rouse. "Dimensions of Native American Stereotyping." *American Indian Culture and Research Journal* 11 no. 4 (1987): 33–58.

———. "American Indian Stereotyping, Resource Competition, and Status-based Prejudice." *American Indian Culture and Research Journal* 15 no. 3 (1991): 1–18.

Harris, LaDonna, Stephen M. Sachs, and Benjamin J. Broome. "Wisdom of the People: Potential and Pitfalls in Efforts by the Comanches to Recreate Traditional Ways of Building Consensus." *American Indian Quarterly* 25 no. 1 (2001): 114–34.

Herring, Joseph B. *Kenekuk, The Kickapoo Prophet.* Lawrence: University Press of Kansas, 1988.

Hirschfelder, Aelene B. *American Indian Stereotypes in the World of Children.* Metuchen NJ: Scarecrow Press, 1982.

Holm, Tom. "Patriots and Pawns: State Use of American Indians in the Military and the Process of Nativization in the United States," in *The State of Native America: Genocide, Colonization, and Resistance,* ed. M. Annette Jaimes, 345–70. Boston: South End Press, 1992.

———. *Strong Hearts Wounded Souls: Native American Veterans of the Vietnam War.* Austin: University of Texas Press, 1996.

Humfreville, James Lee. *Twenty Years Among Our Hostile Indians.* New York: Hunter and Co., 1903.

In the White Man's Image. Video in the PBS series *The American Experience.* 60 min. 1991.

Isaacs, Harold R. *Idols of the Tribe: Group Identity and Political Change.* New York: Harper and Row, 1975.

Jacobs, Margaret D. *Engendered Encounters: Feminism and Pueblo Cultures, 1879–1934.* Lincoln: University of Nebraska Press, 1999.

John, Elizabeth. *Storms Brewed in Other Men's Worlds.* College Station: Texas A&M University, 1975.

Jones, David E. *Sanapia: Comanche Medicine Woman.* New York: Holt, Rinehart and Winston, 1972.

Kavanagh, Thomas A. *Comanche Political History: An Ethnohistorical Perspective, 1706–1875.* Lincoln: University of Nebraska Press, 1996.

———. *The Comanches: A History, 1706–1875.* Lincoln: University of Nebraska Press, 1999.

Kenner, Charles L. *A History of New Mexican–Plains Indian Relations.* Norman: University of Oklahoma Press, 1969.

Kidwell, Clara Sue. *Choctaws and Missionaries in Mississippi.* Norman: University of Oklahoma Press, 1995.

Leacock, Eleanor Burke. *Myths of Male Dominance: Collected Articles on Women Cross-Culturally.* New York: Monthly Review Press, 1981.

Linton, Ralph. *Acculturation in Seven American Indian Tribes.* New York: Appleton-Century, 1940.

Lomawaima, Tsianina K. *They Called It Prairie Light: The Story of Chilocco Indian School.* Lincoln: University of Nebraska Press, 1994.

Lurie, Nancy O. "Menominee Termination from Reservation to Colony." *Human Organization* 22 (1972): 257–70.

Marsden, Michael T., and Jack G. Nachbar. "The Indian in the Movies," in *Handbook of North American Indians*, ed. William T. Sturtevant, 4:607–16. Washington, D.C.: Smithsonian, 1988.

Martin, Joel W. *Native American Religion*. New York: Oxford University Press, 1999.

McBeth, Sally J. *Ethnic Identity and the Boarding School Experience of West-Central Oklahoma American Indians*. Washington, DC: University Press of America, 1983.

McFee, Malcolm. "The 150% Man: A Product of Blackfoot Acculturation." *American Anthropologist* 70 (1978): 1096–1103.

Meriam Report: The Problem of Indian Administration. Washington, D.C.: Institute for Government Research, 1928.

Mihesuah, Devon A. "American Indian Identities: Issues of Individual Choices and Development." *American Indian Culture and Research Journal* 22 no. 2 (1998): 193–226.

———. *American Indians: Stereotypes and Realities*. Atlanta: Clarity Press, 1996.

———. *Cultivating the Rosebuds: The Education of Women at the Cherokee Female Seminary, 1851–1909*. Urbana: University of Illinois Press, 1993.

———. *Indigenous American Women: Decolonization, Empowerment, Activism*. Lincoln: University of Nebraska Press, forthcoming.

———. *Natives and Academics: Researching and Writing About American Indians*. Lincoln: University of Nebraska Press, 1998.

Miller, Christopher. *Prophetic Worlds: Indians and Whites on the Columbia Plateau*. New Brunswick, NJ: Rutgers University Press, 1985.

Mooney, James. *The Ghost-Dance Religion and the Sioux Outbreak of 1890*. Part 2 of *Annual Report of the Bureau of Ethnology, 1892–1893*. Washington, D.C.: Government Printing Office, 1896.

Neeley, Bill. *The Last Comanche Chief: The Life and Times of Quanah Parker*. New York: Wiley, 1995.

Noyes, Stanley. *Los Comanches: The Horse People, 1751–1845*. Albuquerque: University of New Mexico Press, 1993.

Noyes, Stanley, and Daniel Gelo. *Comanches in the New West: 1895–1908*. Austin: University of Texas Press, 1999.

Nye, Colonel W. S. *Carbine and Lance: The Story of Old Fort Sill*. Norman: University of Oklahoma Press, 1937.

Perdue, Theda. *Cherokee Women: Gender and Culture Change: 1700–1835*. Lincoln: University of Nebraska Press, 1998.

Peroff, Nicholas C. *Menominee Drums: Tribal Termination and Restoration, 1954–1974*. Norman: University of Oklahoma Press, 1982.

Philip, Kenneth R. *Termination Revisited: American Indians on the Trail to Self-Determination, 1933–1953*. Lincoln: University of Nebraska Press, 1999.

Powers, Marla N. *Oglala Women: Myth, Ritual and Reality*. Chicago: University of Chicago Press, 1986.

Pritzker, Barry M. *A Native American Encyclopedia: History, Culture, and Peoples*. New York: Oxford University Press, 2000.

Stahl, Robert J. "Farming Among the Kiowa, Comanche, Kiowa, Apache and Wichita." Ph.D. diss., University of Oklahoma, Norman, 1978.

Stedman, Raymond William. *Shadows of the Indians: Stereotypes in American Culture.* Norman: University of Oklahoma Press, 1982.

Stewart, Omer. *Peyote Religion: A History.* Norman: University of Oklahoma Press, 1987.

Stockel, Henrietta. *LaDonna Harris: A Comanche Life.* Lincoln: University of Nebraska Press, 2000.

Stonequist, Everett. *The Marginal Man: A Study in Personality and Culture Conflict.* New York: Russell and Russell, 1937.

Thornton, Russell. *American Indian Holocaust and Survival: A Population History Since 1492.* Norman: University of Oklahoma Press, 1987.

Thrapp, Dan L. *Encyclopedia of Frontier Biography: In Three Volumes.* Vol. 2. Glendale, CA: Arthur H. Clark, 1988.

Trennert, Robert A. *The Phoenix Indian School: Forced Assimilation in Arizona, 1891–1935.* Norman: University of Oklahoma Press, 1988.

Wahhahdooah, Harry, ed. *Deyo Mission.* Lawton, OK: C & J Printing Co., n.d.

Wallace, Edward S. "Ranald Slidell Mackenzie, Indian Fighting Cavalryman." *Southwestern Historical Quarterly* 59 (January 1953): 378–96.

———. "Prompt in the Saddle: The Military Career of Ranald Slidell Mackenzie." *Military History of Texas and the Southwest* 9 no. 3 (1971): 161–90.

Wallace, Ernest, and E. Adamson Hoebel. *The Comanches: Lords of the South Plains.* Norman: University of Oklahoma Press, 1952.

Webb, Walter Prescott. *The Great Plains.* Lincoln: University of Nebraska Press, 1981.

Yellowbird, Michael. "What We Want To Be Called: Indigenous Peoples' Perspectives on Racial and Ethnic Identity Labels." *American Indian Quarterly* 23 no. 2 (spring 1999): 1–22.

Index

Sacred Feathers
The Reverend Peter Jones (Kahkewaquonaby)
and the Mississauga Indians
By Donald B. Smith

Grandmother's Grandchild
My Crow Indian Life
By Alma Hogan Snell
Edited by Becky Matthews
Foreword by Peter Nabokov

Blue Jacket
Warrior of the Shawnees
By John Sugden

I Tell You Now
Autobiographical Essays by
Native American Writers
Edited by Brian Swann and Arnold Krupat

Postindian Conversations
By Gerald Vizenor and A. Robert Lee

Chainbreaker
The Revolutionary War Memoirs of
Governor Blacksnake
As told to Benjamin Williams
Edited by Thomas S. Abler

Standing in the Light
A Lakota Way of Seeing
By Severt Young Bear and R. D. Theisz

Sarah Winnemucca
By Sally Zanjani

CPSIA information can be obtained at www.ICGtesting.com
Printed in the USA
LVOW13*0351190813

348521LV00002B/54/P